Accompanied by sound disc.
Inquire at the Multimedia Center
Service Desk.

A HISTORY OF THE PORTUGUESE FADO

For Judy

Unidentified Fadista in Lisbon, 1950s

A History of the Portuguese Fado

Paul Vernon

Ashgate

Aldershot • Brookfield USA • Singapore • Sydney

The publishers and author acknowledge financial support from **Portugal 600**

and M|C
MINISTÉRIO DA CULTURA

The author has asserted his moral rights.

Published by
Ashgate Publishing Limited
Gower House
Croft Road
Aldershot
Hants GU11 3HR
England

Ashgate Publishing Company
Old Post Road
Brookfield
Vermont 05036-9704
USA

British Library Cataloguing-in-Publication data

Vernon, Paul
    A history of the Portuguese Fado
    1. Fados – History
    I. Title
    781.6'269'009

Library of Congress Cataloging-in-Publication data

Vernon, Paul
    A history of the Portuguese fado / Paul Vernon.

    Includes bibliographical references, discography
and index.
    1. Fados–History and criticism.   2. Folk music–Portugal–History
and criticism.   3. Folk songs, Portuguese–Portugal–History and
criticism.   I. Title.
    ML3719.V47   1998
    782.42162'691–dc21   97–45087
                                CIP
                                MN

ISBN 1 85928 377 2

Typeset in Sabon by Raven Typesetters, Chester and printed in Great Britain on acid-free paper at The University Press Cambridge

Contents

List of plates

Frontispiece: Unidentified Fadista in Lisbon, 1950s (author's collection)

Chronology

This concise socio-political chronology of Portuguese history is intended to provide a contextual setting, with particular attention paid to events of the twentieth century.

2000 BC–200 BC	Evidence of Neolithic settlements, followed by Verracos, Castro Culture and Celts.
210 BC–60 BC	Romans penetrate the area; settlements at Lisbon, Beja, Évora, Santarem.
409–11	Barbarian invasions.
585	Visigoth invasions.
711–16	Moorish invasions.
1095	Henry of Burgundy, upon his marriage to Teresa, daughter of the King of León, is granted the county of Portucale, a strip of land stretching from the Minho river in the north to Coimbra in the south. He ascends the throne with a mandate from his new father-in-law to take as much land from the Moors as he can. Henry is the first monarch of the House of Burgundy.
1112	Afonso Henriques I ascends throne.
1139	Victory of Afonso Henriques over Moors at Ourique; Coimbra established as capital of Portucale.
1143	Afonso Henriques recognized by the Treaty of Zamora as the first King of Portucale.
1147	Afonso Henriques takes Lisbon from the Moors following a seventeen-week siege.
1162	Afonso Henriques takes Beja and Évora from the Moors.

1179	Papal recognition of Portugal as a kingdom.
1192	Earliest surviving evidence of Portuguese as a written language.
1195	Sancho I ascends throne.
1211	Afonso II ascends throne.
1212	First parliamentary assembly at Coimbra.
1223	Sancho II ascends throne; drives Moors from Alentejo.
1248	Sancho abdicates; Afonso III ascends throne; kingdom extended to Algarve, Moors finally conquered. Present Portuguese boundaries established.
1279	Diniz I ascends throne; undertakes constitutional and social reform.
1290	First university established at Lisbon.
1294	Commercial treaty negotiated with England.
1297	Diniz signs the Treaty of Alcañices with Spain, ensuring recognition of Portuguese borders.
1307	First university established in Coimbra.
1325	Afonso IV ascends throne.
1344	Lisbon damaged by earthquake.
1357	Pedro I ascends throne.
1367	Ferdinand I ascends throne; last monarch of the House of Burgundy.
1383	Death of Ferdinand; revolution against monarchy.
1385	João I ascends throne, first elective monarch of the House of Avis. Portuguese and English forces defeat Castilians at Aljubarrota.
1386	Treaty of Windsor confirms Anglo-Portuguese alliance.
1387	King João I marries Philippa of Lancaster, daughter of John of Gaunt of England.
1411	Castilian war ends.
1415	Campaign in Morocco led by Henry the Navigator, son of João, including capture of Ceuta.
1419	Discovery of Madeira.

1422	Seat of government moved from Coimbra to Lisbon.
1427	Discovery of the Azores.
1433	Eduardo I ascends throne; Cape Bojador discovered.
1434	First African slaves brought to Lisbon.
1438	Afonso IV ascends throne.
1445	Senegal discovered.
1446	Guinea discovered by Nuno Tristão.
1457	Discovery of Cape Verde islands.
1465	Probable birthdate of Gil Vicente, Portugal's first great literary figure.
1471	São Tomé and Principe islands discovered by Pedro Escobar and João Gomes.
1474–6	Portugal involved in Castilian succession dispute; defeated at Toro.
1481	João II ascends throne.
1482	Portuguese explorers reach the African Congo region.
1491	First Portuguese settlers arrive in the Congo region.
1493	Bill of Demarcation, agreed between Portugal and Spain, gives Portugal all discoveries east of a meridian 100 leagues west of Cape Verde.
1494	Treaty of Tordesillas with Spain moves meridian to 370 leagues west of Cape Verde.
1495	Manoel I ascends throne.
1496	Manoel orders the expulsion of Jews from Portugal.
1497	Cape of Good Hope and passage to East Indies discovered by Vasco da Gama.
1498	Mozambique discovered by Vasco da Gama.
1500	Brazil discovered by Admiral Pedro Alvares Cabral, 22 April.
1505	Mozambique colonized by Portuguese settlers. Goa discovered.
1509	Portuguese explorers reach Malacca.

1510	Albuquerque captures Goa.
1512	Portuguese dominion in Malay Archipelago founded.
1517	Commercial relations begin with China.
1520	Tower of Belém, in Lisbon, built.
1521	João III ascends throne.
1531	Beginning of the Inquisition.
1537	Lisbon University transferred to Coimbra.
1542	Commercial relations begin with Japan.
1557	Sebastião I ascends throne. Macao comes into Portuguese possession.
1578	Sebastião II, last monarch of the House of Avis, ascends throne; defeated and killed in battle at Alcácar-Quivir; succeeded by his apparently senile uncle, Cardinal Henrique.
1580	Cardinal Henrique dies without heirs, leaving a power vacuum.
1580	Phillip II of Spain defeats Portuguese in battle, seizes Portugal, and is crowned King Felipe I of Portugal, bringing all of the Iberian Peninsula under Spanish rule.
1602–20	Loss of Portuguese settlements in India to Dutch, loss of Malay Archipelago to English.
1628	English college for Roman Catholics established at Lisbon.
1640	Portuguese assert independence from Spain through revolution. João IV, first monarch of the House of Braganza, ascends throne. War with Spain continues.
1656	Afonso VI ascends throne.
1659	Portuguese defeat Spanish at Elvas.
1662	Portuguese independence recognized by English when Charles II marries Catherine of Braganza. Bombay and Tangier transferred from Portuguese to English possession as part of Catherine's dowry.
1663	Portuguese defeat Spanish at Ameixial.
1664	Portuguese defeat Spanish at Ciudad Rodrigo.
1665	Portuguese defeat Spanish at Vila Viçosa and Montes Claros.

1668	Treaty of Lisbon ends war with Spain.
1678	Establishment of port wine trade in Oporto.
1683	Pedro II ascends throne.
1703	Methuen Treaty with England renews Anglo-Portuguese alliance but unfavourable terms badly damage the important Portuguese cloth trade.
1706–1730	João V, aged 17, ascends throne. The discovery of precious metals and gems in Brazil ushers in a period of extreme wealth for the Portuguese empire. João squanders vast amounts of money in huge building projects, almost bankrupting the country in the process.
1731	Work begins on water aqueduct through the Alcántara valley.
1750	José I ascends throne. Marquis of Pombal becomes influential prime minister.
1755	Chartered company formed to regulate Oporto's port wine trade.
1755	1 August; huge earthquake and tidal waves virtually destroy Lisbon and kill thousands.
1758	Marquis of Pombal orders the execution of much of the aristocracy and the expulsion from Portugal of all Jesuits following an assassination attempt on the king.
1761	Black slaves receive emancipation.
1777	Maria I and Pedro III ascend throne.
1786	Pedro dies, leaving Maria sole monarch.
1792	Maria's son John appointed regent due to Maria's deteriorating mental condition. National Theatre of S. Carlos built in Lisbon.
1793	Portugal joins the war against Napoleonic France.
1796	National Library founded.
1801	War with Spain.
1807	Treaty between France and Spain partitions Portugal; French armies enter Portugal. Royal family and court escape to Brazil. French General Junot enters Lisbon and deposes Portuguese royal family.

1808	Portuguese rise against French; Wellington's armies come to assistance of Portuguese and are victorious at Vimeiro. Convention of Cintra evacuates French from Portugal.
1809	French re-invasion; taking of Oporto by Napoleon's armies, recaptured by Wellington.
1810	French take Almeida but are defeated at Battle of Busaco.
1811	Defeat of French at Fuentes d'Oñoro. End of war.
1815	Brazilian colony declared a 'kingdom'.
1816	João VI ascends throne in exile, enraging Portuguse opinion.
1820	Oporto 'Liberal Revolution'; first elections held.
1821	Royal Family returns to Portugal. King João promises to obey the new, liberal constitution.
1822	In Brazil, Dom Pedro, eldest surviving son of King João, chosen as 'Perpetual Defender' by National Congress, 13 May. Brazilian independence proclaimed 12 October.
1826	Death of King João VI; King Pedro IV ascends. Institutes 'Constitutional Charter' 29 April. He returns to Brazil, leaving 7-year-old daughter, Maria da Gloria, on the throne, with her uncle Miguel acting as Regent.
1828	Dom Miguel, backed by military and clergy, proclaims himself King. Pedro, backed by British troops, re-enters Portugal and restores Maria to the throne. He subsequently dies. Political turmoil follows. Government alternatively in the hands of two opposing political groups, Carlists and Septembrists.
1832	Pedro IV sails with expedition from Belle-isle, takes Oporto and proclaims himself regent.
1833	Miguel's squadron taken by Admiral Napier off Cape St Vincent. Duke of Cadaval evacuates Lisbon, queen proclaimed and enters Lisbon.
1834	Miguel renounces claim to throne by Agreement of Évora Convention; civil war ends with liberal victory and exile of Dom Miguel. Royal decree, 28 May, demands dissolution of religious orders, nationalization of church property and seizure of all church monies, which were then applied to the national debt and the establishment of the Library of the

Academy of Science in Lisbon. Death of King Pedro. Queen Maria II ascends to throne.

1836	Revolution in Lisbon, abolition of constitutional charter and proclamation of 1822 constitution. Opening of the National Library in Lisbon. First recorded evidence of the existence of the Fado as a song form.
1838	First worker's association, 'Sociedade de Artistas Lisbonense', established. New constitution formed by Septembrists.
1841	Construction of Alto de S. João cemetery.
1842	Successful revolt in favour of Carlists. Beginning of Costa Cabral parliamentary dictatorship.
1843	Maria II and her German consort Fernando II hold the throne.
1846	Revolt of Maria da Fonte; civil war. Bank of Portugal founded. National Theatre of Queen Mary opened in Lisbon.
1847	Convention of Gramido imposes peace upon Portugal with the threat of foreign intervention if it is not kept.
1848	Gas lighting installed in central Lisbon; Roçio paved.
1852	Direct suffrage established by the Regenerators. Queen sanctions revision of the Charter by the Cortes. Abolition of death penalty for political crimes. Construction of ring road begun in Lisbon.
1853	Death of Queen Maria II; Pedro V ascends throne.
1854	'Hunger riots' due to crop failure.
1856	Cholera epidemic. First railway line, Lisbon-Carregado, opened in October.
1857	Yellow Fever epidemic. Quarantine station opened on south bank of Tagus. Electric telegraph in Lisbon.
1858	Death of Queen Estefania.
1859	Metric system introduced.
1861	Death of King Pedro V. King Luís I ascends to throne. Riots in Lisbon over suspicious death of king.
1863	Abolition of primogeniture. Opening of Archeological Museum in Lisbon.

1864	Portugal signs frontier treaty with Spain in September. The newspaper *Diario de Noticias* founded in Lisbon.
1865	International Industrial Exposition held at Oporto.
1867	Death penalty abolished; civil code published.
1868	Lisbon Water Co. founded.
1869	Abolition of slavery throughout Portuguese territory.
1872	Worker's Fraternity Association founded.
1873	Strikes, in Lisbon and Oporto.
1875	Workers' Socialist Party founded.
1876	Construction on the Maria Pia bridge in Oporto begins.
1878	Census figures: 4,550,699 total including Azores and Madeira. Population of Lisbon, 498,059; Porto, 461,881; Coimbra, 292,037. Illiteracy estimated at 3,751,774
1879	Beginning of construction of Avenida de Liberdade in Lisbon.
1881	Formation of Republican Party. Construction of the Dom Luís bridge in Oporto begins. Strikes in Lisbon and Oporto. Census figures: 4,708,178 total; population of Lisbon, 518,884; Porto, 466,981; Coimbra, 307,426.
1884	National Museum of Fine Arts and Archeology opens in Lisbon.
1885	Death of King Fernando II. Lisbon Penitentiary completed.
1886	Convention of 12 May assigns boundary lines to Angola.
1887	Treaty with China allows continued Portuguese possession of Macao.
1888	Slavery abolished in Brazil.
1889	Death of King Luís I. King Carlos I ascends throne, 19 October. Brazilian revolution deposes Dom Pedro II and declares Republic. Electric lighting in Avenida de Liberdade. Dispute with England regarding Angolan borders. Birth of António de Oliveira Salazar, who will become leader of Portugal 1932–68.
1890	British issue ultimatum over Angola. Countrywide demonstrations. National anthem 'A Portuguesa' composed by Alfredo Keil. Coliseu dos Recreios (Entertainment Coliseum) opens in Lisbon.

1891	Military revolution in Porto, January. Republic proclaimed. Treaty with England, 11 June, settles disputes over Angolan and and Mozambiquan borders. First trams run in Lisbon. Estimated 3000 inhabitants of African descent in Lisbon and Oporto.
1892	Campo Pequeno bullring inaugurated. New Atlantic harbour construction begins in Leixoes, four miles north of Oporto.
1896	First cinema films shown in Lisbon, June. First Portuguese-made film shown in Oporto, 12 November.
1897	Foundation of both the Ethnological and the Geographical Museums in Lisbon.
1899	'Hunger law' enacted; first Portuguese film production company, Portugal-Filme founded in Lisbon.
1900	First gramophone records made in Oporto.
1901	Electric tramway network started in Lisbon.
1902	Electric street lighting extended in Lisbon. Tagus railway bridge opened.
1903	King Edward VIII of England and King Afonso XII of Spain visit Portugal; peasant insurrection at Fundão, January; military mutiny in Lisbon, April.
1904	First cinema – Salão Ideal – opens in Lisbon.
1906	Typographers strike; act defining port wine is passed. First cinema in Oporto opens.
1907	King Carlos dissolves the National Parliament.
1908	Proletariat uprisings; royal family withdraw to Vila Viçosa. Attempt to set up Republican regime fails. Royal family return to Lisbon. King Carlos and Crown Prince Luís Filipe shot by assassin in February. 18-year-old Manoel II ascends to throne.
1910	Proclamation of republic at Lisbon town hall on 5 October. Dr Teófilo Braga appointed provisional president. Manoel dethroned, 10 October, and exiled.
1911	First Republican constitution approved, 20 August. Voting franchise for all males over 21 years. Dr Manoel de Arriaga appointed president 24 August. Church and state separated. Start of sporadic Royalist risings. Universities at

	Lisbon and Oporto established. National Museum of Contemporary Art opens in Lisbon.
1912	Bolshevik revolution suppressed, January.
1914	Outbreak of European war. Portugal adheres to British Alliance but remains uninvolved.
1915	Lisbon bombarded by Germany, 14 May. Dr Teófilo Braga re-appointed president, 29 May. Dr Bernadino Luís Machado Guimarães appointed president, 5 October.
1916	Germany declares war on Portugal, 9 March, following seizure of German ships in Portuguese ports. Portuguese expeditionary force joins allied forces on western front in France. Military revolt.
1917	Following successful liberal revolution, Dr Sidónio Pais appointed president, 11 December. First film studio, Invicta-Filme, built in Oporto. 'The Miracle of Fatima' allegedly takes place, 13 May. In October thousands gather to witness further alleged miracles.
1918	Radical fleet bombards Lisbon 8 January. Sidónio Pais assassinated, 14 December. Admiral João do Canto e Castro Silva appointed president 16 December.
[1918–19]	Influenza epidemic takes 100,000 lives.
1919	Unsuccessful monarchist uprisings in Oporto, Jan/Feb. Dr António José de Almeida appointed president, 5 October. Total value of all Portuguese exports £24,874,650, total value of all imports £52,110,675.
1921	Population of Lisbon 489,600; of Oporto, 203,000.
1925	Dr Bernadino Luís Machado Guimarães appointed president 25 December.
1926	Military coup, 28 May, dissolution of Parliament, provisional government appointed 1 June. Marshal António Fragoso Carmona appointed president 29 April. Beginning of military dictatorship. Press censorship. Salazar appointed minister of finance but resigns shortly after.
1927	Sporadic unrest in Lisbon and Oporto throughout the year.
1928	General Carmona appointed President, Salazar re-appointed minister of finance, March.
1930	Social unrest. Technical university opened in Lisbon;

Government passes law removing all non-Portuguese words from public places and replacing them with Portuguese. This affects all non-Portuguese commercial trademarks. Population of country, 6,654,815; Lisbon, 594,390; Oporto, 215,625; Coimbra, 20,841.

1931   Currency officially stabilized 9 June. Legal Deposit system instigated by the Government requires a copy of all publications in Portugal to be lodged at the National Library. Central Municipal Library in Lisbon opens. First Portuguese sound film, *A Severa*, made in Paris.

1932   Finance minister Salazar offered prime ministership and accepts, 5 July.

1933   New constitution approved, 19 March. Inception of Estado Novo (New State), essentially a benign form of fascist dictatorship. Tobis-Klangfilm builds the first cinematic sound stage in Lisbon. *A Canção de Lisboa* is the first Portuguese-made sound film.

1935   Political parties banned by Salazar's government. Foundation of National Union. Secretariat for National Propaganda established.

1936   Tacit support from Salazar's government for Franco in Spanish civil war. Government-backed *Emisora Nacional* Radio begins broadcasting.

1937   Survey reveals 210 cinemas in Portugal, of which 185 are wired for sound. Opening of the Tauromachian Museum of bullfighting at Campo Pequeno, Lisbon.

1938   Creation of the Instrumental Museum at the National Conservatory of Music in Lisbon.

1939   Outbreak of war. Portugal remains neutral. Lisbon an open city; allied and axis personnel move freely.

1940   Portuguese World Exhibition celebrates foundation of nationality and restoration of independence. Lisbon Academy of Science publishes definitive and simplified Portuguese vocabulary, with government endorsement.

1941   Josephine Baker appears in Lisbon cabaret.

1942   Release of *O Patio das Cantigas*, the most influential and enduring Portuguese comedy film. Brazilian Academy of Letters, using 1940 Lisbon model, publishes simplified Brazilian vocabulary.

1944	60,000-seat National Stadium opens in Lisbon.
1945	Dissident group in Brazil fails in its attempt to redefine Brazilian vocabulary within more traditional parameters.
1947	Cinema audience attendance figures (CAAF): 20.9 million.
1948	Museu de Arte Popular inaugurated. Salazar government sets up National Cinematographic Fund. Lisbon population: 800,000.
1949	Decree prohibits further registration of prostitutes and brothels. Portugal joins NATO alliance.
1950	Population of Lisbon, 1,226,815; Coimbra, 432,044; CAAF, 20.6 million.
1951	Death, in office, of General Carmona. Marshal Francisco Higino Craveiro Lopes appointed president 22 July. Decree of 9 May merges all leases and concessions for Portuguese railways into a single concession granted to Companhia dos Caminhos de Ferro Portugueses. On 11 June all Portuguese colonies reclassified as 'overseas territories'. Monumental Theatre opens in Lisbon.
1953	Opening of University Hospital in Lisbon. Opening of the College Museum of Decorative Arts in Lisbon.
1955	CAAF, 25.9 million.
1956	Television broadcasting begins.
1958	Humberto Delgado runs as presidential candidate; vicious electoral process invalidated. Rear Admiral Américo de Deus Rodrigues Tomás elected president 9 August.
1959	Work begins on Lisbon underground railway.
1960	Humberto Delgado assassinated. Population, including Madeira and Azores, 8,889,331; Lisbon, 1,382,959; Oporto, 303,424; Coimbra, 46,313. CAAF, 26.6 million.
1961	War in Angola begins. All Africans in Portuguese Territories granted Portuguese citizenship. Goa invaded by Indian troops on 18 December and forcibly incorporated into Indian Union.
1962	Brothels closed by government order.
1964	Customs duties between Portugal and its overseas territories abolished.

1965	Rear Admiral Tomás re-elected 9 August. Figures indicate 29 daily newspapers, 449 cinemas and 550,490 telephones country-wide. Population of Portugal 8,525,500; Lisbon, 802,400; Oporto, 303,000 Coimbra, 45,500. CAAF, 25.7 million.
1966	Salazar Bridge across river Tagus in Lisbon opens. Prison population 8114.
1968	Salazar leaves office following brain damage sustained in a domestic accident. Succeeded by Marcelo Caetano.
1970	Death of Salazar. CAAF, 28 million.
1971	Portuguese Institute of Cinema inaugurated. Population est. 9,500,000; Lisbon, over 1m.
1974	Revolution of 25 April led by Major Otelo Saraiva de Carvalho. A bloodless coup establishes the Movimento das Forças Aramdas (MFA) as the ruling party. Collapse of regime. End of censorship. A period of political instability follows.
1975	Angola and Mozambique proclaimed independent. Military coup fails. CAAF, 41.6 million.
1980	Dr Sa Carneiro creates the Democratic Alliance. CAAF, 30.8 million.
1983	Mário Soares, leader of the Socialist Party, is elected prime minister.
1985	CAAF, 19 million.
1986	Mário Soares becomes president. Portugal enters the EC.
1987	Social Democrats take power.
1988	General strike, March; fire destroys much of the old Chiado district of Lisbon, 25 August.
1990	CAAF, 11 million.
1993	First privately-owned televison broadcasting begins.
1994	Cultural Exposition, 'Lisboa '94'.
1996	Exhibition 'Fado, Voices and Shadows' held at Lisbon University.
1998	Expo '98 held in Lisbon.

Preface

In 1987, in a second-hand shop in San Francisco, I found a clutch of gritty, unsleeved 78rpm records on an enticing array of labels and in a language I didn't immediately recognize. Their exotic appearance induced me to buy them and when, that evening, I sat down to play them the music I heard filled me with a strange mixture of responses. It excited me more than anything had ever done since I first heard the Blues as a teenager. It raised goose-bumps on my flesh, offered a sense of *déjà vu* that was mystifying, filled my head with a barrage of questions and left me with a longing to know more. My first introduction to the Fado, therefore, was purely accidental, but I knew then that the quest to discover more about it would be deliberate.

The following day I went to the old San Francisco Public Library, where, in the back stocks, I found more than 200 books on Portugal, many over 50 years old. I read voraciously for weeks, absorbing everything I could about the people, the history, the politics, the economics and, most especially, the music of that country. I began to draw some tentative conclusions and realized that the 27 records I owned represented a surprisingly good introduction to the various styles I was reading about. I had music from the 1920s to the 1950s, Fados from Lisbon and Rio de Janeiro by both men and women, vocal and instrumental pieces from Coimbra and Porto, and local recordings made in Oakland. Twelve weeks after finding the records I arrived in Lisbon, slightly amazed at my own rash behaviour but suspecting, increasingly, that chasing the Fado was going to be a lifelong occupation. The results of my decade-long efforts are offered here, not as the last word on the subject, but as an interim report on a work in progress, and an introduction for readers to a world that I hope will fascinate them as much as it fascinates me.

Paul Vernon

Acknowledgements

This book would not exist without the full and unstinting co-operation of the following people:

Bruce Bastin, for allowing me free and full access to his collection of 78rpm records;
Michael Collins, of Portugal 600, without whom this project would never have even begun;
Ruth Edge, Head of EMI-Archives at Hayes, Middlesex for allowing me to conduct research and handle precious original material;
Ronald Louis Fernandez, for information on instruments;
Nigel Gallop, for allowing me access to his father Rodney's original papers.

My thanks are also due to the following people and organizations, who have all contributed in a variety of ways to the creation of this book:

Ian Anderson; Anglo-Portuguese Society – London; Manoel Baptista: BBC Gramophone Library – London; Bibliothèque National – Paris; William Breslin; British Embassies at Lisbon, Paris & San Francisco; British Library – London; Pedro Caldeira Cabral; Salvador Caiado; Rui de Carvalho; Valentim de Carvalho Lda. – Lisboa; Manoel Cascereigo; Professor Salwa El-Shawan Castelo-Branco; Keith Chandler; João Manoel Caramalho De Melo Domingues; Discothèque National – Paris; Sherwin Dunner; Judy Rolph Ebner; Dr. Janet Topp Fargon; FNAC – Paris; Folk Roots-London; Benno Haupl; Joseph C. Hickerson; Interstate Music – UK; Jack's Record Cellar – San Francisco; Lakme & Company – San Francisco; Library of Congress, Office of Folklife – Washington, DC; Livraria sa da Costa Editoria – Lisboa; Dr. Rainer Lotz; Marie-Loure Manigant; Rachel Lynch; Anita Moreira-Silva; José Mocas; Musical Traditions – London; Diane Napier; National Sound Archive – London; Rui Nery; Jorge Neves; Portuguese Continental Union of the USA; Portuguese Embassy – London; José Reis; Graça Almeida Rodrigues; Tony Russell; Howard Rye; San Francisco Public Library; San Leandro Portuguese Society; Santa Cruz Public Library; Carlos Serra; Ken Smith; Smithsonian Institute – Washington, D.C. ; Richard K. Spottswood; Keith Summers; João Belchior Viegas; Anne Waterfall; Westminster Music Library – London.

And finally, the Purple Heart Thrift Store in San Francisco, where my journey began.

Introduction

The Fado is a strophic song-form peculiar to Portuguese culture, sung equally by both sexes and accompanied almost exclusively by two stringed instruments, the guitarra and the viola. The lyrical content of the Fado is of paramount importance, and the ability of the singer to communicate a range of emotions through the lyrics lies at the very heart of the genre. Fados emanating from Lisbon can be broadly divided into three main subject groups: love, jealousy and passion; celebrations of local areas such as Alfama and Mouraria; and songs about Fadistas and the history of the Fado. Beyond these lie an array of sub-texts and ancillary topics including social comment, humour, family life, personal honour and self-esteem. Anything, in fact, can be a topic for a Fado – Rodney Gallop, during his two and a half year sojourn in Lisbon, found topics varying from the sinking of a British submarine to the death of a footballer through food poisoning. Every Fado must, however, contain two essential ingredients: poetry and saudade.

In much the same way as African-American Blues, the Fado acts as a cathartic release for intense human emotions. But behind this lies a rich panoply of poetic vision and a complex cultural history, the detailed truth of which has often been obscure to all but a few enthusiasts.

In seven short verses Frederico de Brito, one of the major songwriters in the Fado tradition, captured the spirit of the Fado:

BIOGRAFIA DO FADO

They ask me about the Fado
I knew the man:
He was a drunk and a tramp
Who hung out in the Mouraria

He was at least as scrawny
As a greyhound dog
But he claimed to be a nobleman
Because he frequented noble folk

His father was a foundling
Who set sail across the sea
On the ships of Vasco da Gama.
A scruffy, unkempt fellow,

1

A swaggerer more than a Sailor,
Of the old days of Alfama.

Yes I know well where he was born,
And I know he was just a commoner
Who always put on airs
I know as well that he was one of those
Who never knew his parents
Nor had a certificate of birth.

They ask me about the Fado
I knew the man:
Forever a reckless sort,

A faithful friend of disorder
Who'd enter the Moorish quarter
In the dead of night
And, opening up the half doors,
Be king of that drunken night

He went to the cattle drives,
He was a celebrated knight
He was delerium at the carnival
And all that agitated life.

He, who came from nothing
In his nothingness was all.

Joaquim Frederico de Brito[1]

De Brito understood that romantic myth is an integral ingredient of the Fado. In personifying Fado as a 'drunk and a tramp' from the Mouraria who claimed nobility but was unaware of his lineage, he has consciously blended historical evidence with fable and popular conception.

Any Fadista – Fado singer or aficionado – will claim that the lyrical content, whatever its subject, is poetic. Fado's geographical and cultural origins, however, are another matter entirely, and it seems that general agreement about them cannot be reached. Many believe that the origins of the Fado lie in the song of the Portuguese mariner, as de Brito suggests, but it has also been claimed as Brazilian, African and Moorish. Its true home, according to Lisbon traditionalists, is the old Mouraria district of Lisbon; others claim it is in the Alfama, or the Bairo Alto, in the heart of the city. Most agree that it was originally the song of the poor and the dispossessed, but for a few it is the exclusive province of privileged young men and university professors. For some it has been a music associated with a café society lifestyle, while others have only ever experienced its theatrical persona.

'Fado' (from the Latin *fatum*) existed as a term long before the song form took root. The 1891 edition of Alfred Elwes' *Portuguese-English dictionary*,[2] a British publication, defined the word as simply 'fate, destiny'. James L. Taylor's 1970 American *Portuguese-English Dictionary*[3] goes a little further. In addition to Elwes' definition, Taylor adds 'Popular (usually plaintive) song or melody'.

In his description of a night in a Lisbon Fado house, Lawton McCaul noted 'we realize that the Fado can be more than just a song sung at midnight when the lights are low.'[4] McCaul hints at the ability of the Fado to reflect the depths and some of the apparently conflicting aspects of the Portuguese character. Pinto de Carvalho, in 1904, wrote:

> Both words and music reflect the abrupt turns of fickle fortune, the evil destiny of the unfortunate, the irony of fate, the piercing pangs of love, the poignancy of absence or despair, the profound sobs of discouragement, the sorrows of Saudade, the caprices of the heart, and those ineffable moments when the souls of lovers descend to their lips and, before flying back on high, hover for an instant in a sweet embrace.[5]

'Saudade' is inextricably linked with the Fado. Indeed, it could be said that saudade is the very soul of the music. It has no direct translation; Elwes describes it as 'longing', Taylor, more satisfactorily, as 'memory embued with longing; fond rememberence; nostalgia; homesickness'. At its heart also lies the yearning for that which might have been but was not. A poignant nostalgia for unrealized hopes and dreams. In the words of Aubrey Bell:

> The famous saudade of the Portuguese is a vague and constant desire for something that does not and probably cannot exist, for something other than the present, a turning towards the past or towards the future; not an active discontent but an indolent dreaming wistfulness.[6]

Rodney Gallop, the most perceptive English writer on the subject, while quoting Bell, adds:

> In a word, saudade is yearning; yearning for something so indefinite as to be indefinable; an unrestrained indulgence in yearning. It couples the vague longings of the Celt for the unattainable with a Latin sense of reality which induces realisation that it *is* unattainable, and with the resultant discouragement and resignation.[7]

No Fadista of calibre is without saudade and no audience of aficionados will tolerate the absence of it. A saudade-free performance will be rudely halted by a hostile and unforgiving crowd. Saudade must be experienced in order to measure its full impact and, heard once, is then instantly recognizable.

It has to be recognized that the Fado is not universally regarded in the Lusophone world as a defining cultural expression. Many Portuguese, over the last century and a half, have demonstrated emotions ranging from indifference to outrage when confronted with the Fado. In 1926 José Caiel Ribeiro Fortes expressed the opinion that 'It is a song of rogues, a hymn to crime, an ode to vice, an encouragement to moral depravity, an unhealthy emanation from the centres of corruption, from the infamous habitations of the scum of society'.[8] Alberto Pimentel added, rather colourfully, that the songs were 'Immoral melodies ... to be understood only by those who vegetate in the mire of crapulence'.[9]

Nor is Fado the only Portuguese music worthy of consideration. The vibrant folkloric tradition, classical works, 'Musica Populara Portuguese', and new compositions within the contemporary framework are all a part of the mosaic of Portuguese music. This volume attempts only to pay homage to a specific song form that, in the opinion of the author, provides a clear window through which to view aspects of the Portuguese soul.[10]

Notes

1. *Biografia do Fado*, lyrics by J.E. de Brito, 1930s.
2. Alfred Elwes (1891), *A Dictionary Of The Portuguese Language In two Parts*, London: Crosby, Lockwood & Son.
3. James L. Taylor (1970), *A Portuguese–English Dictionary*, Stanford UP.
4. Lawton McCaul (1931), *Portugal For Two*, NYC: Dodd Mead & Co.
5. Pinto de Carvalho (1904), *Historia Do Fado*, rep. 1984, Lisbon: Contexto.
6. Aubrey Bell (1915), *Portugal and the Portuguese*, pub. UK.
7. Gallop, Notes on Portuguese Character (1931) (unpublished), Foreign Memo no. 55.
8. José Caiel Ribeiro Fortes (1926), *O Fado*, Oporto.
9. Alberto Pimentel (1904) *A Triste Canção do Sul*, Lisbon.
10. For further information on other forms of Portuguese music, see Grove: *Dictionary of Music & Musicians and Folk Roots* (various issues from 1992).

1 The Beginnings

Of all the musical forms that could be described as 'urban folk music'[1] – American blues, Greek rebetika, Argentinian tango, Cuban rumba – the Fado is arguably the oldest. The first evidence of its existence as a musical form is to be found in an anonymously published broadsheet from 1833 containing these lyrics:

> We dance the Fado for the fine dance that it is
> And we take a Fadista who knows how to use his knife.

The elements that would create the Fado, however, existed in Portuguese culture long before the publication of this broadsheet. Pinto de Carvalho, writing in 1904, insisted that it had been born on the high seas:

> The Fado is of maritime origin, an origin which is confirmed by its rhythm, undulating as the cadenced movements of the wave, regular as the heaving of a ship, or as the beating of waves upon the shore.[2]

José Régio wrote:

> Fado was born on a day when the wind hardly stirred
> And the sea vanished into the sky
> On a sailing ship's rail, in the breast of a sailor who sang because he was sad.
> 'Portuguese Fado', José Regio/Alain Oulman (undated)

In doing so he propagated the Pinto de Carvalho myth that seafarers were the inventors of the genre, which in itself is a legitimate use of the Fado.

While there is no doubt that Portuguese sailors sung the Fado, they were not the exclusive inventors of the genre. However, Carvalho's book was the first in print on the subject and remained unchallenged for some years. Subsequent twentieth-century research has undermined Carvalho's opinions, producing a more complex picture of Fado's development.

In 1786 António da Silva Leite published 'Estudo de Guitarra em que se expose o meio facil' in Porto, and current research indicates that this is the earliest of all guitarra instruction manuals. Three years later 'Arte de Viola' by Manoel da Paixão Ribeiro appeared in Coimbra. The existence of these books on their own proves little other than the recognition of the two principal instruments of the Fado before the end of the eighteenth century; they must, however, be viewed as part of a wider cultural development.

In a society where the individual voice has difficulty making itself heard any other way, a Fado is often the only platform for opinion. The Fado itself is often the subject:

One day I passed, on the old Rua de Palma,
A certain dark fadista.
A man with a small mouth and a mocking air.
And my soul was at once enthralled.

'Ai, Mouraria', Frederico Valeiro (undated)

Vanquished souls, lost nights, strange shadows in the Mouraria.
A whore sings, guitars weep, ashes and fire, pain and sin
All of this is sad, all of this is Fado.

'All This is Fado', Anibal Nazaré F. Carvalho (undated)

The popular folk quatrains of the Portuguese are rooted in a love of poetry that can be traced back to at least 1189, through the survival of a poem by Pay Soarez de Taveiroos. Throughout the following 600 years Portuguese culture nurtured vibrant poetic tradition. There were Cantigas D'Amor (love songs), Cantigas D'Amigo (songs of feminine lovesickness), Cantigas D'Escarnho e de Maldizer (songs of ridicule and invective), Bailadas (dance songs), and songs of and by rural workers, mariners, pilgrims, fishermen and prisoners. By the time the Da Silva Leite and Ribeiro books were published, these songs were an integral part of Portuguese life. However they, like the instruments, were not so much the roots of the Fado as ingredients that would lie inert until events forced a blending process to occur in Lisbon.

Portuguese-African slaves, liberated in Lisbon in 1761, settled in the Mouraria and Alfama districts where, among other activities, they danced the Fofa and the Lundum. Dezetoux provides the only known contemporary description:

The people ran about here and there singing and dancing the fofa, a sort of national dance performed in pairs to the accompaniment of the guitar or some other instrument; a dance so lascivious that decency blushes at witnessing it.[3]

Most 'decent' Portuguese apparently blushed in sympathy with Dezetoux, and King Manoel the first issued a decree banning the dancing of not only Fofas but also Lundums, Batuques and Charambas – all Brazilian imports. The Lundum was danced as widely as the Fofa in the Lisbon of the early 1800s and it is probable that it crossed the Atlantic with returning black employees of Portuguese entrepreneurs. Both dances were accompanied by the Spanish guitar, referred to by the Portuguese as the viola.

The influence the Africans had on the development of the Fado might have been minimal had they not mingled freely in the Alfama and Mouraria with their economic peers, a specific Portuguese underclass known as 'Fadistas' (implicitly, 'fatalists'), regarded as unsavoury and dangerous characters. The first known description of them appears in an 1849 novel:

A young man of about 19 or 20 years old, wearing a short jacket, a tilted hat, a rolled, silk belt in the manner of a Fadista, muddy cotton trousers, smoking his 5 reis cheroot.[4]

From 1874 we have a further description by the English Lady Catherine Jackson:

> Fadistas wear a peculiar kind of black cap, wide black trousers with close fitting jacket, and their hair flowing low on the shoulders.... They are held in very bad repute, being mostly vauriens of dissolute habits.[5]

An undated, but evidently early nineteenth-century print depicts a Fadista fitting Lady Jackson's description dancing the Lundum; the most direct surviving evidence we have of the cultural exchanges that occurred between the freed slaves and the Fadistas.

Both Lundum and Fofa, therefore, were guitar-accompanied dances performed in and around the Mouraria and Alfama by Africans and Fadistas alike. To this equation we may now add the Modinha. In essence, the Modinha is a song-form with similarities to the popular quatrain. Again, its origin seems to be Brazilian – certainly it was, like the Lundum, appearing on Brazilian gramophone records at the beginning of the twentieth century – and it is very likely that it furnished the basis for the lyrical structure of the early Fado, providing the key ingredient as it metamorphosed from a dance into a song.

William Beckford, an eighteenth-century English traveller, offers us a contemporary impression of a Modinha that would fit the Fado itself:

> Those who have never heard this original sort of music, must and will remain ignorant of the most bewitching melodies that ever existed since the days of the Sybarites. They consist of languid interrupted measures, as if the breath was gone with excess of rapture, and the soul panting to meet the kindred soul of some beloved object. With a childish carelessness they steal into the heart, before it has time to arm itself against their enervating influence; you fancy you are swallowing warm milk, and are admitting the poison of voluptuousness into the closest recesses of your existence. At least, such beings as feel the power of harmonious sounds are doing so; I won't answer for the hard-eared, phlegmatic northern animals.[6]

Writing in 1904, Pimentel observed:

> The national plays performed in the Salitre and Rua dos Condes theatres contained Italian music, the most catchy airs of which become public property and were transformed into the modinhas which radiated all over the country. In these pieces were also interpolated Lundums, African dances which served as interludes. Gradually the Lundum began to take on an independent existence as a song which rapidly became the favourite of the lowest grades of society who gave it the name of Fado.[7]

It seems likely that the term 'Fado', as specifically applied to the newly-emerging song-form, took its name from the Fadistas who practised it, rather than the reverse, as has often been previously assumed. To the masses that seethed through the Alfama and Mouraria may now be admitted Pinto de Carvalho's beloved sailors, clearly participants in the development of this emerging music rather than sole inventors. In his seminal work *Portugal – A Book of Folkways*, Rodney Gallop added;

> There is nothing inherently improbable in the suggestion that the Fado is a sort of musical half-breed, heir to the rhythmic features of one parent and the melodic features of the other.[8]

What the Fado needed at this stage was a celebrity, someone to whom the Fadistas could relate and whom the middle-class and aristocracy could easily blame. A colourful figurehead, a *tabula rasa* who would represent, positively or negatively, what anyone wanted the Fado to be. That celebrity was Maria Severa.

The only reliable information concerning the real – as opposed to the legendary – Maria Severa is that contained in her death certificate. She was born Maria Severa Honofrianna in 1820 – the month remains unknown – and died of apoplexy 26 years later, on 30 November 1846. During that quarter century she defined the Fado and fixed it in the public imagination by dint of her association with Comte (count) de Vimioso, an aristocrat and bullfighter with a deep affinity for slumming. Her death certificate baldly adds that she was a spinster and a prostitute and that she was buried, without a coffin, in a common grave. There is no reliable contemporary illustration of her, but there are many artistic interpretations, displaying her as a short, plump, round-faced young woman, an image which has endured ever since.

Contemporary accounts place her as the daughter of a tavern owner known as 'The Bearded Lady' in the Madragoa area of Lisbon. When she was about 20 years old – possibly earlier – she and her mother moved into a tavern in the Rua da Capalão in the Mouraria, where she became embroiled in the world of the Fadista. This world was surveyed in 1840 by Dr. Inácio dos Santos Cruz who noted:

> In the different parts of the city where there are the greatest numbers of low prostitutes – such as Rua da Esperança, Travessa do Pasteleiro and Ruas das Madres and Vincent Borga; in (the) Bairro Alto (in) Travessa dos Fieis de Deus, Poco da Cidade etc, there are taverns which are regularly frequented by these prostitutes and the low orders who are in the habit of associating with them. The busiest taverns are chosen, and to attract still more customers the taverners encourage the prostitutes and allow the most obscene language and all manner of indecent and disreputable behaviour. Many a dance and bacchanal has been accompanied by shameless and lascivious acts....[9]

It is said of Severa that she took a lover (his name has not survived) who was transported to Africa for an unspecified crime, and that she pined for him and, in doing so, honed her expertise as a singer of Fado.

The Conde de Vimioso's reputation as a successful and glamorous bullfighter drew admiration from the crowds who frequented the bullring, crowds that were drawn from every level of Portuguese society; from aristocrat through merchant to Fadista. Bullfighting in Portugal differs from its Spanish counterpart in one essential aspect: the bull is not killed, but taunted to the point of exhaustion and then removed from the ring. The reputation of a Portuguese bullfighter rests therefore upon his survival skills and his style, rather than his ability to commit a *coup de grâce*. The Conde de Vimioso liked to celebrate his victories by drinking and carousing in taverns, and it is claimed that he discovered Maria Severa playing and singing a Fado in her mother's tavern during one of his post-fight celebrations. At this point fact and legend fuse immutably. The two reportedly reacted to one another immediately and passionately. Most accounts mention Severa's 'tempestuous' nature and allude to an emotionally unstable relationship between the two lovers, charged with a great sexuality.

The story of Severa and Vimioso is that of a classic doomed relationship; the Comte's family would never allow him to entertain any thought of marriage to a woman of Severa's social standing and, inevitably, he left her to follow his aristocratic destiny. She, in a fit of morbidity, ate and drank herself to death, finally choking on a surfeit of pigeon and red wine. The veracity of this melodramatic ending is difficult to ascertain as no hard evidence exists other than the death certificate's reference to apoplexy.

What really happened matters little. Severa's story gripped the public imagination immediately; it was widely and colourfully reported in newspapers, discussed at every level of society and celebrated in song. As a result, not only was Severa catapulted to posthumous celebrity, the Fado itself gained the first broad public attention it had received outside of its own narrow world. Pinto de Carvalho notes that the Fado 'appeared on the streets of Lisbon after 1840'[10] which would roughly coincide with the explosion of publicity that Severa and Vimioso generated. Maria Severa became the keynote figure of Lisbon Fado, celebrated in many songs, in novels, plays, stage musicals and, in 1931, 'A Severa', the first Portuguese sound film. To this day, women Fadistas will don a black lace shawl in her honour before singing. How musically talented Severa may have been is, of course, impossible to determine and perhaps of less significance than the popularity she attained. Her role as martyr in a form of music that celebrates martyrdom is now unassailable.

From the middle of the nineteenth century the Fado's profile grew steadily. The song 'Fado Choradinho' (Fado of the Unfortunate) was registered in Lisbon in 1850. César Neves notes that: 'This is one of the real, true Fados and one of the oldest on which many later ones were based'[11] adding in the same volume that a version of 'Fado da Severa', dating from the middle of the nineteenth century, 'Is the basis of all Fados which lament fate and were listened to rather than danced to'.[12] This, too, corrobates the suggestion that Fado made a transition from dance to song.

Looking at the latter half of the nineteenth century further indications of the existence and use of the Fado emerge. Several cartoons, drawings and portraits celebrate the Fadista of the period. An 1857 print, 'The Sailor' by E. J. Maia, portrays a dark skinned man playing the guitarra; from 1859 Maia's 'The Boy And The Blind Man' depicts street musicians playing guitarra and viola, the first visual evidence of what was to become the classic instrumental accompaniment to the Fado. An 1872 Indian-ink drawing by Rafel Bordalo Pinheiro shows us an image of a Fadista very close to Lady Catherine Jackson's description, with a bottle and glass at his side, playing a guitarra. The following year Pinheiro portrayed 'The Fadistas', a pair of apparent drunks, one singing, one playing the guitarra.

By the 1880s cheap song books had started to appear. 'The Good Fadistas Almanac' of 1885 is regarded by collectors as seminal. It contains 32 songs arranged for guitarra and proves conclusively that the structure of the Fado was fully formed by that date. By the 1890s the Fado, in a somewhat stylized form, had reached the middle-class theatre stage. As early as 1869 the *revista* (review) 'Ditoso Fado' had been performed at the then newly-opened Teatro da Trindade, a neo-romantic theatre with a seating capacity of 800. No record of the content of this show has survived but in all probability it was much the same as those reviews performed from the turn of the century onwards (see Chapter 2). In bringing the Fado off the street and out of the tavern these early theatrical productions set in motion a chain of events that would turn full circle in the next fifty years, as we shall see in more detail later.

Notes

1.   Rodney Gallop (1931), Some Records of the Portuguese Fado, *The Gramophone*, October.
2.   Pinto de Carvalho (1904), *Historia Do Fado*, rep. 1984, Lisbon: Contexto.
3.   Dezetoux, quoted by Gallop in *Portugal – A Book of Folkways*, Cambridge: CUP.
4.   Quoted in Pinto de Carvalho (1904), *Historia Do Fado*, op. cit.
5.   Lady Catherine Jackson (1874), *Fair Lusitania*, London.
6.   William Beckford (1928), *Travel Diaries*, London.
7.   Alberto Pimentel (1904), *A Triste Cançao do Sul*, Lisbon.
8.   Rodney Gallop (1936), *Portugal – A Book of Folkways*, Cambridge: CUP.
9.   Dos Santos Cruz, quoted in Pais de Brito's *Voices and Shadows* (1994), Lisbon: Electra.
10.   Pinto de Carvalho (1904), *Historia Do Fado*, op. cit.
11.   Neves, quoted in *Voices and Shadows* (1994), Lisbon: Electra.
12.   Ibid.

2 The Instruments

The Portuguese guitarra, the most fundamental of all instruments within Fado, is a member of the cittern family. Early citterns, usually flat-backed stringed instruments with four or more double courses of metal strings and a body narrower at the bottom than the top, were prevalent throughout Europe from at least the fifteenth century, and may date back to as early as the thirteenth century as there is evidence, among miniatures made by King Afonso II (1186–1223) that survive, of stringed instruments not dissimilar to the Henriquez guitarra being played in pairs.

By the eighteenth century the design of the standard cittern had altered somewhat; its body, while remaining flat-backed, had become pear-shaped, and it was being referred to as a 'guitar'. The modern Portuguese guitarra has as its direct ancestor an eighteenth century English guitar, first mentioned in print by António da Silva Leite in 1796.[1] Leite published an instruction manual in that year for the 'Guitarra Portuguesa', in which he wrote that the instrument had been imported from London where it was being made by a Mr Simpson, and that from Simpson's pattern, guitarras were being constructed in Portugal by Luís Cardoso Soares Sevilhano. Leite's book is the first published evidence of the development of a specifically 'Portuguese' guitar.

In the hands of Portuguese makers, the instrument underwent some alteration. From surviving examples held in museums and private collections we can chart the progress of Portuguese guitarra making.[2] Two guitarras supposedly belonging to Maria Severa (1820–1846) have survived. The earliest, made by Joaquim Pedro dos Reis in 1764, is a pear-shaped instrument with six double courses of metal strings, 17 frets and a circular soundhole. It is built with wooden tuning pegs arranged in Spanish style, with six pegs either side of the head. The second, from 1773, is essentially the same design, but with a slightly narrower body. As guitarra design evolved, the distinctive shape of the modern instrument steadily emerged, but it was not until the end of the nineteenth century that the characteristic metal fan-shaped tuning head, often known popularly as a 'turkey's tail', appeared.[3] Nineteenth- and early twentieth-century illustrations and photographs depict Fadistas playing both early and late versions of the instruments; the 'Good Fadistas Almanac', a song-book from 1885, features a drawing of a musician with an early instrument, as does a photograph of a female street singer from about 1920, but by the time the Fado had reached the first stages of professionalism, the fan-shaped machine head was the dominant design, as evidenced in José Malhão's 1910 painting 'O Fado'.

The design of the new machine-head allowed the player easy access to each of the twelve threaded metal rods that governed the tuning, as they fanned out over 60 degrees, providing convenient gaps that enabled the thumb and forefinger to grasp and turn the screw thread on each shaft. It also provided the instrument with a unique trade mark that has endured throughout the century and become a key facet of Fadista imagery.

The modern Guitarra Portuguesa, almost unaltered in design from the late nineteenth century, is an unusually strong and flexible instrument. It is often constructed from rosewood, cypress, mahogany or sometimes maple sides and a spruce or pine face. The fingerboards are in either ebony or rosewood, and the neck cedar. Simple and relatively inexpensive examples will feature little ornamentation, but especially fine models can be stunningly beautiful, with inlaid mother-of-pearl designs around the soundhole and along the fingerboard, and sometimes an ornamental head, either a flat teardrop style or a design known as a 'caracol' (snail) protruding from the back of the neck and reaching out and over the machine head. The caracol on Armandinho's instrument, as the quotation from Lawton McCaul mentioned in Chapter 3, was carved into a nude figure. The modern instrument is played with 'unhas' – literally, fingernails – finger picks that follow the natural curved line of a human nail, rather than the right-angle protrusions employed in, say, American folk guitar traditions.[4] These unhas are taped to the thumb and index finger, allowing the player to use rapid strokes that would otherwise be impossible without damaging the fingers, and enable the accomplished musician to produce complex and cleanly-picked instrumental passages. The size of a guitarra tends to vary with the locality in which it is built. Those made in Lisbon are actually the smallest, those from Coimbra the largest, while those made in Porto sit somewhere between the two. The difference is minimal, often less than a few centimetres overall, but the Coimbra Fadista will almost never be seen employing a Lisbon-style guitarra, and *Fadistas de Lisboa* will generally refuse to play a Coimbra instrument.

The position, almost exclusively a male one, of the virtuoso guitarra player in Fado is one of some complexity. He is expected both to conserve tradition and be innovative; he must breath new life into old themes; he must compose and improvise; he must be able to accompany a wide range of vocal talent; he must understand every nuance of the Fado but not be bound by it. Salwa El-Shawan Castelo-Branco, writing in 1994, expressed the opinion that the development of Fado accompaniment upon the guitarra could be divided into two periods, pre- and post-Armandinho. In the period before Armandinho the accompaniment was limited to simple harmonic schemes; and creative playing within the context of a sung Fado grew directly out of Armandinho's influential style.[5]

An in-depth analysis of early Fado recordings, which has only been possible during the last few years, adequately supports Castelo-Branco's theory. Prior to the influence of Armandinho's innovative approach, the great bulk of recorded vocal Fado from Lisbon was indeed accompanied effectively but very simply. Little embellishment or creative improvisation was heard within the framework of the song. After about 1930, Armandinho's influence, both as a recording artist and as a regular accompanist at the Luso Fado house, permeated Lisbon's Fadocentric society. Other guitarristas began emulating his approach and, often, his style, producing a heavily embellished sound that has now become characteristic of contemporary Fado.

A modern Fado will invariably open with an instrumental passage of anything from four to sixteen bars, during which the tempo and melody will be established. As the singing commences, the guitarrista will subtly alter his position, becoming a 'second voice' behind the vocalist, providing counter-melody and ornamentation. His work appears in the gaps between sung stanzas, and is known as 'contra-canto' (literally, 'counter-song'). This style, pioneered by Armandinho, but bearing the imprint of his mentor Petrolino, was further developed by guitarristas such as Raúl Nery, who brought an astonishing fluidity to the works of the Fadistas Carlos Ramos, Fernanda Peres, Frutuoso França and Amália Rodrigues.

Sometimes a second guitarra is used, accompanying the first instrument in much the same way that that instrument accompanies the singer, providing an 'echo' of the overall sound. The instrument that is invariably paired with the guitarra is known in Portugal as, variously, the Viola, Violão, Viola Francesa or, sometimes, the Viola Espanhola, and is essentially what is commonly known as a Spanish guitar, a standard acoustic six-string instrument with a round soundhole. It was probably introduced into Portugal directly from Spain during the eighteenth century, and was therefore a familiar instrument by the mid-nineteenth century, when Fado was emerging. It is almost never used for instrumental solos of any length; instead, it will supply the steady rhythmic pattern that provides a solid backdrop against which both the guitarra player and singer can perform. Sometimes, especially in Rio de Janeiro from about the early 1940s and Lisbon from approximately ten years later, a Viola Baixo, or bass guitar, will also be added. This is a large acoustic four-string instrument, roughly half as big again as a viola, resembling the Mexican Bajo Sexto, and it performs the same function as an upright bass. The single virtuoso figure in Viola Baixo playing is Joel Pina, whose steady yet flexible rhythm has graced many live performances and recordings since the early 1950s.

Few other instruments are used for either accompaniment or solo virtuoso performances. In Fado's early theatrical context, and also within the Coimbra tradition, a piano will sometimes be heard, but it will never be found in a Lisbon Fado house and has been little used since the early 1930s. Individual recordings featuring solo performances upon the violin, the saxophone and even the ocarina exist, but they represent novelty value only.

A Fado heard today in a typical Lisbon Fado house will invariably be accompanied be either a duo of guitarra and viola, a trio of either guitarra, viola and viola baixo or two guitarras and a viola, or a quartet of two guitarras, viola and viola baixo. When you sit down and prepare to listen, it is worth reminding yourself that what you are about to hear is not, in any way, a revivalist experience but the product of over a century and a half of unbroken tradition, innovation and practice.

Notes

1. António da Silva Leite (1786), *Estudo da Guitarra*, Porto.
2. These museums include the Horniman in London, the Victoria and Albert in London, the Royal College of Music in London, the Reed Collection at the University of Edinburgh, the Smithsonian Institute in Washington DC and the Museu de Etnologia in Lisbon.
3. Mascarenhas Barreto mentions this in *Fado; Origens Líricas e Motivacão Poetica*, c. 1910.
4. The use of 'unhas' began in the 1930s when guitarists were forced (by the new professional status acquired in clubs) to play for hours, to entertain customers and please the boss. Then, they could not use the 'broken-nail' argument as amateurs did whenever they were tired of drunken singers and bosses alike.
5. Salwa El-Shaan Castelo-Branco in *Fado, Voices and Shadows*, Lisbon: Electra.

3 Lisbon

The charm of Lisbon is primarily human and only secondarily architectural. Never for one instant are its streets empty of people. Hence, with the help of the southern sunshine, the predominant impression which it leaves is one of seething vitality.

In view of its position as an Atlantic port there is singularly little tang of the sea in Lisbon, save during the summer months when the cool *nortada* wind blows through the city ... it is as though the sea and all that belongs to it recoiled impotently from the hills on which the city is built.

The exploration of these hills is a fascinating pursuit. Each is a maze of narrow winding alleys, steep flights of steps and miniature squares [and] improbably, intervals of horizontality ... The houses in these thickly populated quarters are solid and massive, though often sadly decayed, and this note of vanished splendour is echoed in countless baroque portals and fountains ... The general impression of lightness is enhanced by the square dormer windows and the terra-cotta finials which give a coquettish upward curve to the steep roofs. There is an unreal, almost theatrical quality in these Lisbon slums, especially those of Alfama and Mouraria, which cling precariously to the slopes below St. George's Castle.[1]

The Lisbon that Rodney Gallop encountered in 1931 was essentially the same Lisbon that Maria Severa had known a century before, and the same Lisbon whose heart would burn away in the great fire of 1988. That fire and Portugal's entry into the EC have altered the face of the city more radically than any events since the earthquake of 1755, but for over 150 years the geographical framework in which the Lisbon Fado thrived remained largely unchanged.

By the beginning of the twentieth century, the Fado had become a permanent feature in the everyday lives of Lisbon's working class. Performed in taverns and brothels, at home and on the street, it was used for both cathartic purposes and entertainment, generally at the end of the working day. Joaquim Pais de Brito eloquently described this proto-Fado as being:

Confined to the poor of the city who had no jobs or worked irregularly, loading and unloading down by the river. They lived in a self-protected, enclosed environment, in a labyrinth of old quarters, wrapped in the shadows at nightfall. Words and music emerged in the oral tradition, there were no identifiable or individual lyricists or composers. The themes of the songs were, and continued to be the same as they always had been – destiny or forces beyond man's control; natural disasters, crime, death, heinous and great deeds. These subjects gradually became associated with more specific urban references evoking life in the locality – the streets, taverns, meeting places, and

15

well-known characters, coupled with the latest news of public figures and visitors to the city. At the same time a note of complaint or a sense of loss crept in, accurately reflecting human relationships which were all too frequently violent, insecure and uncomfortable, recounting all forms of love, hate and sexuality.[2]

Love though, in all its many variations, has always been the main theme and the largest platform for poetic writing.

It can be sensual:

> Who taught you to love
> Who taught you kisses
> And with hands
> Taught you to undo
> All of a body's knots
> Opening it slowly.
>
> 'Who Taught You To Love'; Ivette Centeno (undated)

or confidently sexy:

> Put on this red belt to make your waist slender
> I want other women to admire your figure
> I want all your girlfriends to know about us
> In Fado it's already whispered that we're made for one another.
>
> 'The Red Belt', public domain

It can become disillusioned, and often achingly lonely:

> Love is water that passes; everything passes,
> Everyday dies; what does it matter if I die?
>
> 'Love is Water That Passes'; Alfredo Duarte/Augusto
> Cesar Sousa (undated)

> One day you left and the cold, sad wind
> Chased away the spring.
> And then autumn came and the forsaken leaves
> Died waiting for you.
>
> 'Fado of the Rua Defesa'; José Serôdio/
> António Calen (undated)

Hurt and anger too, will surface, occasionally becoming violent:

> Each time I see you I lust to possess your life
> To kiss you and mark the kiss with the point of a jack-knife.
>
> 'A Lust to Possess'; Silva Tavares, 1950s

Sometimes a song of love will have a twist in the tale:

> Slumped against the counter of the inn
> Of sickening hue where worms had done their worst
> The drunken painter with a pencil drew
> The faithful portrait of a woman lost
>
> Shameless, the woman among the uncouth noise
> of glasses clinking and joke on boorish joke
> Clung to the lad and covering him with kisses
> Asked him with smiles what sort of job he did

Risking a stumble, but the risk he took
He told of his profession all self-taught
She listened and immediately knew
How to ask him to draw her tempting face

Her reveller's features on a dirty sheet
The drunken painter with a pencil drew
He touched the profile up and wrote below
In letters none could read, his modest name

The ragged drunkard with the famished face
In a harsh raucous voice he read it to her
She, mad with grief, towards the young man came
Kissing his face and then embracing him

She was the painter's mother and all or most
Moved and amazed before that strange new picture
While the poor artist crumples up the drawing
Of the faithful portrait of a woman lost.

'The Drunken Painter'; Henrique Rego/Alvaro
dos Santos, 1930

Often a sense of triumph over adversity will emerge. But in the end, it is a simple matter of bowing to the inevitable, eternal truth – the acceptance of *saudade*:

To depart is to stretch our arms, reaching for the unreachable dreams
Whose destiny is to remain
Dying, a man's suffering ends, but departure is too much to bear.
It's a grief far worse than death.

'To Depart Is To Die a Little'; António Santos/
Mascarenhas Barreto (undated)

There is always, however, a final word:

And on closing these verses
Sung in a minor key
It is fitting that we honour
The singer's drunken spree.

'Closing'; Fernando Pessoa (undated)

Nevertheless, Fado developed on more than just a street level. By 1907 it had reached the attention of writers and intellectuals, who gathered in that year to pay homage to the memory of Maria Severa. They 'legitimized' the genre for themselves and their peers with the simple act of acknowledgment, and went further by attempting to promote it as a vehicle for poetic and philosophical endeavour. They also assisted in polarizing public opinion, not only between intellectuals and grass-roots supporters (de Brito's 'poor of the city', some of whom felt their music had been hijacked), but between different factions of the intellectual bourgeoisie. A third group, professional empresarios, singers, actresses and actors, saw it as an opportunity to mount middle-class entertainment that would bring people into the theatre. By 1910, three levels of Portuguese society were claiming the Fado as exclusively theirs.

For the working classes, the Fado continued to supply music for everyday life.

Blind beggars, who could find no other work and who received nothing from the government save an official black wooden begging box, regularly sang and played guitarra on the streets for a few escudos – a practice which could still be found as late as the 1980s – and their role in the dissemination of the Fado has been a key one. Sometimes shepherded by family members but, more often than not, young orphan boys, they were mobile enough to spread the Fado both within and beyond the city; they went south to Estoril, Setúbal and Faro, they drifted north to Porto and the rich vineyards that lay inland of it. The partnership of blind singer and boy became an interdependent unit. The youth, acting as the 'eyes', also sold sheet music to supplement their meagre income.

In this way isolated communities were exposed to the emergent Fado both in terms of printed music and live music, the musicians leaving eager amateurs in their wake. A first-hand account of one such singer, written by the English travellers Jan and Cora Gordon in 1933, survives:

> One morning, in search of a sketch, we were wandering by the high columns into the valley. Near the centre a pipe allows a trickle of water to drip into a trough for thirsty animals. Here, squatting in the shadows, we saw a family with a covered mule-cart.

> 'Look!' exclaimed Jo. 'Those people have guitars!'. There were two men, two women, and some children; the older of the men was engaged in tuning a Portuguese guitarra. They returned our salutations with proper ceremony.

> 'You are musicians?' asked Jo.

> 'The father is blind' replied the younger woman, as though this explained everything, as, of course, it did. In Portugal, as in Spain and, indeed, all along the Mediterranean, the blind have the privilege of begging to music. The Portuguese distinguish between the ones born blind and those blinded. A popular verse says:

> Those born blind
> Sing like birds, day or night
> Those made blind
> Weep only for their sight.

> At last the blind man had his guitarra in tune with his wife's guitar, which in Portugal is called a 'viola'. Then, at our request, they began to play an accompaniment and an obbligato, while the round-cheeked daughter sang a Fado.
>   As they had printed broadsheets for public sale we acquired a specimen, and so can give a rough translation of the mote and half of the first verse. Published at Estremoz, it bore the reassurance, 'Passed by the Censor'.

> Barbarous and murderous mother,
> Pitiless and heartless, she
> Threw her daughters down a well,
> Where they died in misery.

> Her husband ran away to sea,
> Three long years an ocean ranger,
> Yet she managed to conceive
> Twins by some ungodly stranger.

> With a quaint yet serene and even joyous voice the placid young woman, who herself was clearly 'expecting' in a very short time, sang several verses of this horrific tragedy.

Such strong meat was but a normal sample of their wares. The price of the broadsheet was a penny, and the other songs included were: 'A Wretch Who Killed His Father With a Knife': 'A Brute Who Robbed and Murdered Three Small Girls': 'A Frightful Assassin Who Poisoned Her Husband and Three Sons': and 'The Shame of a Woman with Respect to the Dress Fashions of Today'. We are sure that the last song was the one which the expectant soloist sang with the most genuine feeling:

You can see each little breast
Underneath the flimsy dress
Nor can words of mine express
How the girls show all the rest

What about their skirts cut high
Higher than their garters tie
Stockings reaching to the thigh?
Coliseumward they go
What God gave them that they show.[3]

Rodney Gallop noted that 'the blind guitarists of today have popularised, in every corner of rural Portugal, the urban Fados and the catchy theme-song of the sound-film "A Severa" '.[4]

Fadistas, blind or otherwise, also attended and supplied music for weddings, wakes, birthdays, religious festivals, bullfights, fairs, public holidays and picnics. What they were singing was often an improvisational form of the Fado referred to as the 'decima', a quatrain in ten-line verse form. Using this flexible vehicle, the Fadista was able to extemporize, tell long and complex stories, and engage in verbal duels with other Fadistas or members of the audience. The decima's origins are rural – versions of it spread their history across much of pastoral southern Europe – and its appearance in Lisbon broadly coincided with the migratory patterns of rural Portuguese workers in search of the better life promised by an increasingly industrialized urban milieu. As the Fado settled into the mainstream of Lisbon's workaday life, the popular perception of the Fadista's role subtly altered. Still regarded by many as rough and of loose morals, the term Fadista nevertheless became more closely associated with the music itself. Whereas, 50 years earlier, the Fadista had been viewed principally as a knife-wielding bandit who lived by criminal codes, by about 1900 the perception was more one of a colourful low-life bon viveur, closely associated with prostitution, drinking and, most especially, the Fado.

The Emergence of the Poet-Fadistas

The year 1910 witnessed the exile of the royal family and the establishment of the Republic. It produced an enormous tide of hope, among all but the minority of aristocracy, that living and working conditions would improve radically. This heady atmosphere produced a plethora of new ideals and ideas. Young poets and intellectuals saw in the Fado the opportunity to express themselves in a way that was both traditional and innovative.

In April 1910, just a few weeks before the proclamation of the Republic, the poet Carlos Harrington produced the first issue of the weekly magazine *O Fado*. In July, Raúl de Oliveira and Augusto de Sousa published the first edition of *A Alma do Fado*. Fuelled by a genuine belief in the ability of the people to govern themselves, Harrington saw *O Fado* as a way of reaching the populace through a medium they were already familiar with. The Fado would become the perfect vehicle for reflecting and shaping popular opinion.

Harrington died in 1916, the same year the poets Jorge Gonçalves and Artur Arriegas launched the magazine *A Canção de Portugal*. In 1922 João Linhares Barbosa, who was to become one of the most influential of lyricists, founded *Guitarra de Portugal* and the following year João Reis's *A Canção do Sul* and a different *O Fado*, edited by Manoel Soares and José da Silva (also known as José Bacalhau) reached the newsstands. The regular publication of these magazines not only allowed the poets who ran them the indulgence of their own egos, but also presented the population of a newly-republicanized society with some challenging options. For the first time, a wide and regular circulation of previously unpublished material allowed the working class access to new ideas. The redundant monarchy would have seen this as a dangerous and subversive practice, but with the optimism of a new republic, all things were considered to be possible.

However, philosophical and ideological differences began to surface among the editors and supporters of these publications. Two opposing groups were formed, and by 1923 the split was open and very public. The main bone of contention centred around where the Fado should be sung, rather than what the lyrics might contain or imply. 'Grupo Solidariedade Propaganda do Fado', supported by Soares and da Silva's magazine, felt the music belonged wholly to the people, by which they essentially meant the working classes. They believed that the true home of the Fado lay in the taverns and cafes, and they further defended it against the sometimes virulent attacks launched by the popular press. 'Grémio Artístico do Fado' took the view that it should be performed artistically in drawing rooms, in essence turning it into a form of self-conscious art music.

The poet-editors debated these topics with great ferocity in the pages of their own journals until 1926 when a military coup ousted the government, replaced it with a junta and, among other things, introduced lyric censorship. From that point on many commentators, feeling the spirit of the republic lost and the argument thus rendered pointless, began to change direction. Nevertheless, the legacy of published Fados that they supplied the public created a huge pool of music and lyrics that blended into popular culture and provided accessible material for generations of Fadistas to draw upon.

From 1926, when published and recorded Fados had to be submitted to the government for approval, i.e. were effectively censored, nothing considered political or subversive was allowed to be made public. However, individual tales of human experience, both good and bad, were permissible. Many writers therefore began exploring themes of honour within the family and nobility of spirit among individuals. Family life was a propagandist theme throughout the Salazar years

(1928–68). Great importance was placed upon the strength provided by family and, in turn, the strength that the family gave back to mother Portugal. Acts of kindness, nobility and sacrifice within the family group were often used as allegorical propaganda by the government and reported in the newspapers or on radio as 'human interest' stories. The following example is generic rather than specific, but illustrates the kind of themes that were popular: family love, religion and individual sacrifice.

> When her sick mother did not smile,
> She went out begging and thus said she;
> Our good Lord watches over you
> I'll be back, mummy, pray for me.
>
> Now night comes down and full of fear
> The angel homeward maskes her way
> Clutching tightly to her breast
> A scrap of bread, now stale and dry
>
> On her way home ward she bent down,
> Picked up a scrap of orange peel;
> She chewed it to perfume her breath
> And thus a simple lie she'd tell
>
> All innocent she murmurs soft;
> To see me happy, mummy, eat
> Believe me, I can't be hungry if
> I've had an orange for my sweet
>
> The mother sniffed her little mouth
> And smiling said; You didn't deceive
> Come little well-fed one and eat
> And then I'll eat the bread you leave.

'The Sacred Lie', Carlos Zamura, 1930s

It is interesting to note that the government made no attempt to censor the theme of poverty. Prostitution, long an established facet of urban life in both Lisbon and Porto, was another topic not subject to censorship. Such a course of action would have been practically useless, since poverty and prostitution are daily facts of life, but it highlights the isolationist attitudes of the Portuguese government. It did not occur to them that anyone outside of the Lusophone world would bother to listen to Fado.

With the Poet-Fadistas established as arbiters of taste and fashion, the Fado took a step closer to professionalism. The continued publication of the weekly journals ensured that the Fado stayed in the public arena. Biographies of popular Fadistas, news, interviews and comment from songwriters and pundits were all regular features. Lyrics, although now subject to government scrutiny, were still published. 'A Canção do Sul', especially, became increasingly populist and 'star' orientated, as the memory of the fragile Republic drifted further away under government propaganda.

The Revista

In the theatre, there was little talk of philosophy or poetry. What was important was to keep the doors open and the patrons happy. Fado had been employed by the Portuguese theatre from at least 1869 when the revista (review) 'Ditoso Fado' opened at the Teatro da Trindade. The revista genre is central to the Lisbon theatre tradition. Standing apart from the staged works of the great Portuguese poets and writers, translations of Shakespeare's plays, and the general run of comedy and drama, the revista was often a simple and unpretentious affair, a vehicle for music as much as dramatic content. It was never serious, carried no great political or social message and was deeply loved by the public. An English enthusiast wrote:

> I wish you could see the little revues they put on in Lisbon, quite simply and cheaply pro-
> duced. Your stall costs you a few escudos, but they go with a swing which some of our
> West End managers might envy.[5]

By 1900 the revista was an established and popular form of entertainment for the middle classes. The format for shows like 'A.B.C.'(1905), '30 Dias Em Paris' (1908) or 'Capote e Lenço'(1911), was essentially the same. A large number of songs were woven around a thin plot, often of love found, lost and found again, and set against a background either familiar, like the Mouraria, rustically nostalgic or exotic, like Paris. The programmes comprised not just guitarra accompanied Fados, but also solo ballads and duets in a light operatic format, and interpretations of current dance hits such as the tango or the maxixe, with music provided by a small pit orchestra.

The first decade of the twentieth century represented something of a golden age for the revista. The popularity of its stars rested not only upon their individual theatre performances but also upon the dissemination of their songs via sheet music, and their appearance on the first gramophone records. Already well-loved by the middle-income public, the revista singers' new recordings were enthusiastically received, and little else calling itself Fado was recorded in the first 20 years of the century.

Júlia Mendes (1885–1911), was a comedienne-fadista who, in a brief career before tuberculosis claimed her life, appeared in numerous successful productions including 'P'rá Frente' (1906), 'Ó da Guarda!' (1907) and 'Sol e Sombra' (1910). However, Mendes' major artistic and commercial triumph lay in her interpretation of Maria Severa in the 1909 production of 'A Severa'. She made songs for several record companies in Lisbon between 1905 and her death, accompanied by both orchestra and solo guitarra. Her contemporary, Maria Victoria (1888–1915), recorded just once around 1908 and, like Mendes, died tragically young, also of tuberculosis; her popularity was such that a Lisbon theatre was named after her. Others survived longer, including Angela Pinto (1869-1925) who appears to have gone unrecorded but whose performance in the 1901 production of 'A Severa' is currently believed to be the earliest stage interpretation of the Severa legend.

One of the longest surviving actors was Estevão de Silva Amarante (1889–1951) who began his career at the Teatro Avenida when he was 12 years old, appearing as a variety of child-characters in the production 'A Viagem de Suzette'. He appeared in 'P'rá Frente' with Júlia Mendes when he was 17. By 1916, in 'O Novo Mundo' he had perfected the 'Ganga' (drunkard) routine that would become the keynote of his career. As a singer, he was closer to the spirit of the cafes and streets, as his recordings, even accompanied by a turgid pit-orchestra, testify. 'Fado da Ganga', recorded for Lusofone records, was such a hit that he made two further versions, with different lyrics.

The revistas had the effect of bringing a version of the Fado, albeit bowdlerized, to the middle classes who then claimed it as their own. The sheet music issued at the time, mostly revista hits aimed directly at this audience, was often transcribed not for the guitarra but the piano, since most middle-income family homes had one. Thus, the style of Fado that the different classes chose to listen to became emblematic of their social status. However, the advent of cheap recorded music would begin to blur the distinctions.

Adelina Fernandes and the Early Recording Industry

Working within the traditions of Maria Victoria and Júlia Mendes, the lyric soprano Adelina Laura Fernandes(1896–1983) became, by a combination of artistry, luck and circumstance, a key transitional figure within the framework of the Lisbon Fado. Her first appearance, at the Teatro Apolo in 'Mealheiro' in 1919, reportedly met with enormous success. It featured several songs, notably 'Fado da Saudade', 'Adeus', 'Fado da Idanha' and 'Canção das Perdidas', that remained popular enough to be sung, seven years later, at her first recording session, for Columbia.

Fernandes continued to appear in stage shows, revistas and operettas throughout the 1920s: 'Carapinhada', 'Arco do Cego', 'Chave D'Ouro', 'Maria Rapaza' and 'Prima Inglesa' all kept her busy throughout the decade, but it was one show, the 1926 production of 'Mouraria', that became her best known and loved achievement. Following her first recording session for Columbia, in the summer of 1926, she switched to Odeon for a single release and then, in the autumn, to Homokord, who printed the lyrics of her Fados on the sleeves of her records. However, in the spring of the following year she recorded for Grand Bazaar do Porto on their new and prestigious Gramco HMV series. The following year, she recorded for them again and this time, on 1 October, signed a three-year contract. The contract listed her address as Rua das Taypas 38–2 in Lisbon, and required that she record a minimum of 24 songs a year for three years. She would receive a flat fee of 1500 escudos (nearly £14) per title, a huge sum of money for the period, up to three times more than any other artist was being paid. Clearly, her talents were thought to be worth the money and the surviving evidence of sales figures confirms this. Her records outsold everything else in catalogue, and were spearheading HMV's profile in Portugal.

Consequently, there was some panic in 1929 when it appeared that she might not be able to record:

> As you informed us that the recording period would be held in the beginning of July we had already informed the artists accordingly and now that you inform us that you are prepared to record about the 16th of August, some of the principal artists state that they are engaged for recitals abroad. We got yesterday from the manager of the theatre where Adelina Fernandes is working the information that this company, Adelina included, is sailing for Brazil on the 20th August. We decided at once to cable you as follows:
>
> ADELINA SAILS BRAZIL TWENTYETH AUGUST NECESSARY START RECORDING ABOUT FIRST AUGUST STOP PROGRAMMES SENT TODAY.
>
> As the voyage of Adelina cannot be adjourned we hope you will kindly see the way of anticipating the recording period as much as possible as it would be cause of a great inconvenience if this artist could not make now at least half of the contractual records. She is disposed to give us a letter saying that the remaining titles may be recorded in our next session, which will be after the end of the contractual year. We await your reply.[6]

In the event, 14 recordings were squeezed in over the weekend before the company sailed, thereby allowing HMV to issue songs from Adelina's current hit musical 'Maria Rapaza'. While Adelina was preparing to sail, correspondence was passing between Gramco and the Victor company in Brazil:

> We have been informed that Mme Adelina Fernandes is going to Brazil (Rio and São Paulo) at the end of this month.
>   Mme Fernandes is considered to be the finest Portuguese singing actress and singer of Fados. We have an exclusive contract with her and shall appreciate your kind co-operation in advertising and featuring her records while she is in your territories.[7]

Her appearances in Brazil became a regular fixture for several years, and the Victor company issued over half of her recorded output in both Brazil and North America. She also appeared in Spain, Madeira and the Azores throughout the first half of the 1930s. By 1937, however, the demand for Fernandes records had waned. Her original contract had included a clause that guaranteed her 1500 escudos per title for 24 titles per year whether the company required them or not. Now, with 14 titles left unrecorded, she wrote asking either for a new recording session in order to fulfill the contract, or for the balance of 21 000 escudos, close to £200, to be paid to her. Grand Bazaar were in no position to fund such a session, and the head office at Hayes did not feel her sales potential warranted any new issues. After some haggling, Fernandes and the Hayes Overseas Department agreed that her contract be cancelled without prejudice and that she should receive half the balance contractually owed. Fernandes did not record again, but continued to live and work in Lisbon until her death at the age of 87.

Her impact upon the course of the Lisbon Fado was considerable. She was the first successful singer of the early electric–recording era, and her popularity helped to fuel a demand from the public for the new technology. As the first Fado 'star', her success also legitimized the actress-fadista tradition that would later include Maria Alice, Herminia Silva and ultimately Amália Rodrigues. It also helped break the boundaries between class-determined Fado styles and performers.

Fadistas, especially women, would now start to move more freely between the stage and the emerging professional Fado House circuit.

Some had already begun to do so, including Maria Emelia Ferreira, who had been an understudy to Adelina Fernandes in the theatre. She was among the first wave of Fadistas, in the company of Maria Silva, Ermelinda Vitoria and Madalena de Mello (recorded within months of each other in 1926–27) who sang in a more directly emotive style than had previously been heard on disc. A blending of street-level attack with a measure of professional polish produced a sound with a balanced synthesis that would appeal to a broader cut of the population. Maria Silva, also known as Mariasinha (Little Maria) was a remarkable, metallic-voiced singer whose three-year recording career, for GBDP, earned her the astonishing amount of 1000 escudos per title, fees overshadowed only by those paid to Adelina Fernandes. Silva freelanced in the growing Fado House circuit for some years then relocated to Brazil, where she made a final appearance on record as late as 1957.

Casas do Fado

With the increase in recording and broadcasting activity, the Fado was now reaching a wider audience than it had previously, and the consequent demand created a need for venues where the music could be heard. Entrepreneurs, therefore, started to open establishments where a Fado could be enjoyed by those who did not wish to enter a world of

> Unscrupulous individuals who sing it drunkenly in squalid dives amid the cackling of harlots, barbarically mutilating the language that Castillo, Herculano and Camilo did so much to aggrandise.[8]

Towards the end of the 1920s, the number of cafes and restaurants, now known as 'Casas do Fado' (Fado houses), increased. They ranged from exclusive and expensive to cheap and cheerful; by 1931 they had become an established part of the city's nightlife and were starting to receive non-Portuguese visitors:

> To hold (the Fado) surely in one's grasp it is best to go to one of the popular cafes such as the 'Luso' and the 'Victoria' where it is regularly performed by semi-professional Fadistas.
>   The social standing of these places seems to be largely a matter of headgear. Entrance to the first is forbidden to those wearing caps or berets (a fine distinction). On the other hand, the patrons of the second, mostly seafaring folk, seem to wear no other head-covering. The spacious rectangle of the 'Luso' and the low-vaulted room of the 'Victoria' are alike crowded with tables and chairs at which many men (but few women) sit drinking coffee, beer, or soft drinks with exotic names like Maracuja or Guarana. Presently the lights are lowered and turn red, and a woman steps on to a low platform. She is the singer. Her accompanists, seated in front of her, are armed with guitars of two different types, known the one as the guitarra and the other as the viola. The tune of the Fado, or figured variations upon it, is played on the former instrument which has a sweeter, more silvery tone, while the latter is used to provide a thrumming accompaniment, alternating invariably between chords of the tonic and the dominant seventh.

After a few bars of this accompaniment the Fadista begins her song. With head thrown back, eyes half closed, ecstatic expression and body swaying slightly to the rhythm of the music, she sings in the curiously rough, untrained voice and simple, unpretentious manner which are dictated by tradition. The Fado does not lend itself to bel canto and the opera singer with his cultivated voice and professional manner would never be tolerated by the audience that listens in unbroken silence to these songs.[9]

The Luso was, and would remain, one of the more upmarket restaurants, catering to the middle classes, foreign diplomats and the occasional tourist. The Victoria was a venue more of and for the people, but the Fadistas moved freely between them. An early tourist captured the essence of the latter type of cafe when, in 1931, he stumbled, unprepared, into the Solar de Alegria, a first-floor establishment on the Praça de Alegria:

There are footsteps on the stairs. Enter a jovial young man with a Spanish guitar which has extra bass strings; followed by a slender, keen-faced companion who carries the most fascinating instrument I ever laid my eyes on. They bow, and sit down at the table next to ours – so that, while they smoke and chat, I am given the opportunity to study the looks of this curiosity. It is a Portuguese guitar, about three-fifths the size of the Spanish or Italian kind used in America. The shallow, pear-shaped body is but slightly modified from that of the medieval lute, but there are twelve strings instead of eight; and the 'tuners', instead of being thumb screws at the back, are upright metal rods bristling out at the top in fan formation, like the feathers of a turkey's tail.

Back of these would curl a violin-scroll if this were an ordinary Portuguese guitar, but this happens to be a deluxe specimen (as the gold trophy plate attests); in lieu of the scroll there is a free fantasia of carving, with the prettily wrought figure of a recumbent nude. While I have been noting these technical details, several tables-full have drifted in, each newcomer exchanging greetings with the musicians. An elderly couple, as domestic looking as the characters in a Thrift Advertisement, smile at everybody and take what seems to be their accustomed seats. Certain persons not so respectable also appear, choosing places where they can notice and be noticed. But they seem to be ignored in the clatter of animated conversation. Theirs is a waiting game. Suddenly, at a signal from the musicians, the lights are dimmed to a shadowy blue. In an atmosphere of rapt listening the guitars begin; very softly at first, like the tap dancing of pixies; then swelling to a coruscating brilliance. Listeners lean forward to watch the agile fingers of Armandinho, who makes his guitar sound as though it were an ensemble of several instruments; singing sostenutos and glissandos, overlaid with a dazzling complexity of embellishments; purling tones offset by spirited staccato and lightning-like runs; and, at times the cool ethereal quality of an aeolian harp. The accompanying guitar contributes depth, fullness and accent. Together their playing, varied with subtle light-and-shade and seductive toyings with the time-beat might be described as a kaleidoscope of sound.

Lights and conversation are on again and the musicians have resumed their cigarros, but a senhora and I have not yet come out of the Blue Enchantment. How can such everyday looking young men as these – now chatting with friends and allowing them to 'try' their guitars – how is it possible that they are such great guitarists?

Blue lights again. But this time the tinkling iridescence of the guitars has no sooner sent us dream-gathering than we are startled by the voice of a singer. Startled because we had no inkling that this was to be a song; and even more electrified at the almost feverish intensity of emotion. I can feel tingles running up my spine.

The singer – a pale, dark-haired youth – seems oblivious of his surroundings. Remaining seated, with his back to his audience, he lifts his throat as a thrush does, and sings as Anglo-Saxons cannot or dare not. With us, such ardent expressionism on the subject of love would be considered alarming.

In succeeding 'Blue Lights' other singers take their turn. None of them has a really trained voice, but that seems to be no handicap; for the Portuguese maintain that anyone who 'feels' can sing. And they do, surprisingly, under the witchery of the guitars; so that we find ourselves present at a sort of lyrical Experience Meeting devoted to the religion of inamorata-worship and the pangs thereof.

A young woman is coaxed to the centre of the room. She, poor creature, is obviously a lady of mercenary amour. We wonder what sort of song she will sing. Presumably something night-clubby. But no; it is a Fado about Mary Magdelene who, though a sinner, was forgiven and made a saint. 'Nowhere in this world will you find perfection' runs the song, 'So be not harsh in judging even the worst of sinners for they too are human beings'. Hearing her sing these words – simply, without mawkishness or bathos, and looking straight out over the heads of her listeners – we realize that a Fado can be considerably more than just a song at midnight when the lights are low. In fact, Fados are spontaneous poetry of the human heart, shared with an audience that feels and understands.[10]

Armandinho (1891–1946) was already a legendary figure by the time McCaul's account of him was written. His guitarra style, inspired by the nineteenth-century guitarrista Luís Carlos da Silva, known as 'Petrolino' (a shadowy figure who recorded just once in 1904), and honed by long association with live performance, was more complex and innovative than almost any who preceded him. First recorded by Columbia for Carvalho in 1926 under his real name, Salgado Armando Freire, he went on to perform under his professional sobriquet for Gramco/GBDP two years later, leaving a stunning legacy of instrumental performances. However, from 1930 until a heart attack killed him sixteen years later, his main income was derived from his role as manager of the 'Luso' Fado house, initially located on the Avenida de Liberdade and later at Travessa De Queimada, just off the Rua da Rosa in the Bairo Alto. Supported by the viola playing of Georgino De Sousa, Armandinho nightly accompanied some of the most passionate and well-loved Fadistas of the period.

Berta Cardosa (b.1916), then a teenager, remembers vividly her first meeting with him:

> I began singing because I'd always loved it. My debut was at a party. My brother had taken me to a Fado house and there were a lot of people there. And my brother told the manager, the great Armandinho, the best guitarrista of all time, that I sang really well. I was about 14 or 15 at the time. So I started to sing and everyone was on their feet.
>
> The boss (Armandinho) was ecstatic when he heard me, and he came up to me and said 'Wouldn't you like to come and sing here?' and I said 'Oh, I couldn't, I don't know, I can't sing well enough, and my mother certainly wouldn't let me'. So they went off and then came to talk to my mother. Then they contracted me to go and record in Madrid, and I went.'[11]

The events Cardosa describe took place around early 1930. Certainly by the end of March 1930 Armandinho had written to Gramco at Hayes expressing dissatisfaction with his own recordings and asking for a release from his contract; his hidden agenda being that the rival Odeon company had engaged him as a talent scout and accompanist for its new series of Fado recordings. As the manager of the

Luso, Armandinho was in the perfect position to take up the Odeon offer. In about the spring of 1930 he assembled an astonishing array of talent – all of them 'Luso' regulars – and, with Georginho de Sousa, accompanied them by train to Madrid. Berta Cardosa, along with Lisbon Fadistas Ercília Costa, Júlio Proença, Joaquim Campos, Filipe Pinto, Alfredo Duarte, Leonor Marques and Cecilia D'Almeida, second guitarrista João Fernandes and the Coimbra artist Dr António Menano, all arrived together at Odeon's Madrid studios to record some 50 titles. By the summer of that year the records, distributed by the Sociedade Fonográfica Portuguesa at Rua S. Nicolau 113, and issued in special sleeves featuring photos of the artists, were in catalogue. On 24 September, at the Park on the Avenida de Chelas in Lisbon, Armandinho, De Sousa, Cardosa, Proenca, Pinto, Duarte, D'Almeida and many others appeared in a 'Grand and impressive evening of Fados and songs dedicated to the hard-working people of the Chelas'.[12] More or less the same group appeared in concert three days later at the Alcántara Football Club. D'Almeida, one of the most intense singers ever recorded, died two years later, aged 21. The artists now working regularly were regarded as professional both by themselves and the industry that was growing up around them. Centred upon the Fado Houses, but including concerts, radio appearances, recordings, tours to the provinces and abroad, the growth of this new industry altered the path that the Lisbon Fado was to take. As more Fado Houses opened, the artists were able to move increasingly freely between them; some signed contracts to appear in specific establishments, others freelanced from one club to another. For the first time, the Fado offered more than catharsis and diversion: it became, for a few, the way out of a vicious circle of poverty.

One of the first and most successful Fado singers was Ercília Costa (1902–1986), a fisherman's daughter from the town of Caparica, just twenty miles south of Lisbon. Originally apprenticed to the garment trade, she first sang at the 'Retiro Ferro de Engomar' Fado House when she was still a teenager. By 1930 she had made one solitary record for Brunswick and was appearing regularly at the newly-opened 'Luso':

> You can hear the Fado any evening in Lisbon at one of the numerous cafes where it is sung. The lights go down and a small platform is occupied by three figures. Two of these, seated, play the viola . . . and the guitarra . . . The singer stands behind them and above their steady rhythmic accompaniment sings, in the curiously easy voice and simple unpretentious manner which are traditional, the verses of the Fado. And it is precisely in the manner of singing of Fadistas such as Ercília Costa, which no musical notation, but only the gramophone, can convey, that the chief character and charm of the Fado lie'.[13]

Ercília Costa's career took her to Madeira and the Azores in 1932, accompanied by Armandinho, and Brazil – where her Odeon recordings were widely available – in 1936. There she appeared as the star of the wildly successful 'Companhia de Vasco Santana e Mirita Casimiro' show. Upon her return to Lisbon she reappeared at the Luso, but the following year was singing in Paris at the 'Comedie' club on the Champs-Elysees. In 1939, accompanied by guitarrista

Casimiro Ramos, she journeyed to New York to appear at the Portuguese Pavilion of the World's Fair. Crossing the United States by train, singing for Portuguese communities along the way, she ended up in Hollywood and, although current research fails to unearth any evidence of film appearances, she made a positive impact upon the Hollywood community and became friends with Bing Crosby and Cary Grant. American Columbia also saw fit to issue some of her Odeon recordings to coincide with this tour, even though they were, by then, almost nine years old. During the years 1940 to 1944, when Lisbon was an open city, she again returned to her regular engagement at the Luso, still accompanied by Armandinho and De Sousa, and still sharing the stage with Berta Cardosa, Joaquim Campos, the legendary Alfredo Duarte and a young Amália Rodrigues. When the war ended, she again toured America and then returned to Brazil for a fifteen-month sojourn and eventually retired in 1954 to live quietly in a Lisbon suburb, dying peacefully at home on 16 November 1986. She was, arguably, the first international Fado star, and certainly provided inspiration for future generations of Fadistas.

Those who followed in Costa's footsteps found the Fado house circuit increasingly image-conscious. In an attempt to distance themselves from the old, negative images of the Fado, the more upscale establishments were making concerted attempts to re-shape the context in which the music was presented. The notion of the Fado as authentically and typically Portuguese, inextricably tied to a vaguely rustic-folkloric background, and shorn of any vestige of a Rabelaisian mentality, was widely promoted. To a great degree this fitted neatly into the propaganda that the government – now headed, as it would be until 1968, by Dr Salazar – was promoting and, given that the government now issued music licenses to both Fado Houses and performers as well as vetting lyrics, the Portuguese music industry had good reason to choose this path.

While such pragmatism marginalized the old guard of amateurs who still chose to gather privately and sing the traditional songs, this new situation created an atmosphere of opportunity for performers, songwriters, promoters and restaurateurs alike. By 1936 the 'Retiro da Severa', decorated with fadocentric and folkloric motifs, was advertising that its clientele was composed of 'diplomats and people of distinction'[14] and in the same year they signed to contract a group of the most popular Fadistas including Berta Cardosa, Maria Emelia Ferreira, Adelina Fernandes – now no longer working in the theatre – and Alfredo Duarte (1891–1984), also known as Alfredo Marceneiro.

Though little recorded, Duarte was a major figure in Lisbon Fado circles for over four decades. As a songwriter, he was held in awe by his contemporaries. Freelancing, he appeared regularly at a number of Fado Houses, especially the Luso, Solar de Alegria and Retiro dos Marialuas, throughout the 1930s and into the war years. He also played during the intervals at at least two cinemas, the Chiado Terrasse and the Salão Rex. By trade he was a carpenter, and his craftsmanship earned him the title 'Marceneiro' (Master Carpenter) which became his professional name.

By 1937 the Luso had moved to the Bairro Alto, widened its target audience and was advertising itself as 'the establishment favoured by families.' A year later, the magazine *A Canção do Sul* was publishing detailed instructions on how to decorate a Fado House:

> The decoration must be of popular Lisbon origin: and when it is not of a maritime character it must be of a country nature. The pots of sweet basil, and everything which can signify the adoration of flowers, or evoke the windows and verandahs where the Lisbon woman waits for her Portuguese sailor when she is missing him, are all authentic symbols of the Fado. God bless the decorators who are now working on the refurbishment of certain Fado salons, that they may respect the essential precept of Fado culture.[15]

As the 1930s progressed, the Fado House circuit became more increasingly exclusive in its approach. Not for the first time, the working classes found themselves marginalized. As Rodney Gallop pointed out, entrance to establishments like the 'Luso' was forbidden to those wearing the wrong kind of hat. With professional Fadistas now moving freely between the Fado Houses, theatres, radio stations and recording studios, a new gap developed between the paid artist and the unpaid amateur. There was no question of a lack of saudade or commitment on the part of either group, it was simply a matter of class and economics. In a curious re-shaping of public opinion, the Fado was now:

> Identified with the working-classes, who started to be seen as guardians of tradition, and less as a threat to the institutional order. They were regarded in a new light, and the picturesque image assigned to them was reinforced. It was now possible to give free reign to the expression of nostalgia and transform the Fado into a tradition. The appearance of the Fado Houses as 'typical' restaurants was partly a result of this idealogical approach to the Fado. The degree of authenticity of the reconstructions of this tradition in the Fado-Houses could be determined according to how typical they were. This assessment could now be made with a definite criterion; the more intensely the Fado was able to recreate the 'popular environments', in 'socially dignified' conditions, the more 'typical' and genuine it was.'[16]

From this new position, new stars emerged. Maria Alice (b.1904) had been active since at least the previous decade, recording for Brunswick in 1929. She gained a new recording contract with EMI-Carvalho in 1936, and appeared regularly in the now refurbished Solar de Alegria, an establishment Lawton McCaul would have barely recognized. The *Diario de Noticias*, Lisbon's nightly newspaper, described Alice as an 'Actress-Fadista', a term probably coined by journalists, but an accurate enough description of the new genre of professional female singers who worked both as actresses in the theatre and, more often, as singers in the Fado Houses. This group included Dina Tereza, still trading on her reputation as the star of the 1931 film 'A Severa', and the immensely popular Herminia Silva (1913–1993).

Herminia Silva had started her career in 1926 when she appeared to critical acclaim in the revista 'Mouraria' with Adelina Fernandes. She starred in 'Zé dos Pacatos' in 1934 at the Teatro Trindade and, two years later, made her first records. She was described by Eduard Sucena as a 'comedienne specialising in picturesque language',[17] referring to her ability to twist words and imitate musical instruments, as her interpretation of a trombone solo on the 1945 recording of 'Trompeta' confirms. By 1941 she was a firmly established star, appearing that year in 'A Desgarrada' at the Teatro Maria Vitoria and immediately afterwards in 'A Tendinha' at the same venue.

The years 1940 to 1945 brought a strange ambience to Portugal. With neutral Spain acting as a physical buffer, the reality of events occurring in the rest of Europe seemed remote to the inhabitants of Lisbon. Yet, at the same time, the presence of both Axis and Allied seamen, embassy staff, trade representatives and spies in what was suddenly a strategically important Atlantic seaport, brought a new awareness of international affairs to the city. Both Rádio Berlim and the BBC broadcast nightly Portuguese programmes aimed directly at Lisbon. In a bizarre twist, the two propagandists were to be found advertising their wavelengths on the same page of the *Diario de Noticias*. Financial houses handled transactions for the British, Free French, German and Italian governments and supplied native currency to spies preparing to infiltrate enemy territory. As a free port, Lisbon's docks played host to ships from across the world. The Portuguese government had to tread a fine line, since its benign though essentially fascist philosophy was at odds with its traditional ties with Britain. It therefore granted the British access to the Azores as a submarine base, at the same time allowing the Nazis to buy Portuguese raw materials at favourable rates.

All this activity brought a great deal of money to the city and business boomed. The cinemas, theatres, restaurants and cafes were packed and the Fado Houses played host to a sudden influx of non-Portuguese customers. The war, having given Portugal a new strategic importance, by extension gave the Fadistas a fresh audience. As well as strengthening the economic base of the Fado House circuit, the war also laid the groundwork for the post-war tourist industry by focusing international attention upon it. Herminia Silva's career blossomed during this period. In June 1942 she appeared in cabaret at the Café Latino and the following September saw her star in a new show, 'A Voz do Povo', at the Teatro Maria Vitoria. She now concentrated exclusively on theatre and cabaret work, and stopped playing the Fado Houses. The BBC recorded her in 1946 for a radio documentary as her career continued successfully, and she appeared in the 1947 film 'Um Homem Ribatejo'. She starred in further shows, and made recordings for HMV, Decca and, finally, Melodia.

Although very little recording was undertaken during the war years, one session was arranged by Valentim de Carvalho in the summer of 1942 for the specific purpose of recording Fernando Farinha. Known as 'O Miudo Da Bica'(The Kid from the Bica district), he had won a talent contest singing Fados in 1937 when he was barely nine years old. A contemporary newspaper report noted that 'This boy sings the Fado better than many adults. Let us hope that he does not lose this skill as he grows older.'[18]

Farinha immediately began appearing at the Solar de Alegria and the Retiro de Severa, standing on a stool while performing, so that he could be seen, and in June of that year, was recorded by EMI. At the age of 13 he appeared on the cover of 'A

Canção Do Sul', dressed in a three-piece suit and described as 'Intuição Precoce' (literally 'intuitively precocious'). By the time he was 19 he had been a professional Fadista for a decade and has remained a firm favourite, singing and recording regularly both in Portugal and Brazil. In 1963, still looking remarkably youthful, he starred in the film 'O Muido da Bica', playing a character based upon his own experiences.

Directed by Constantino Esteves, with music by Alfredo Duarte, the film is remarkable for a number of reasons. Although set in a period between the 1930s and 1950s, much of it was shot on location, the unaltered Lisbon landscapes providing an authentic backdrop. In an early scene, a young boy is shown singing at what probably represents the talent contest Farinha won in 1937, much to the disapproval of his stern father, a conservative and hard-working barber, a man whose family home is depicted as humble, clean and well-ordered, but whose own father was a Fadista who wasted his life. When the father suddenly dies, the teenager assumes the mantle of head of the household and begins work in a factory, assembling radios. During the evenings he sings the Fado in a cafe and comes to the attention of a talent scout, suspiciously similar in appearance to Alfredo Duarte. As a result, he turns professional, singing first in a bigger Fado House, then on radio. The new life overtakes him; he distances himself from his neighbourhood sweetheart to carouse the Bairro Alto until the small hours with a fur-clad good-time girl. Drinking more, he becomes a stranger to his mother and younger sister until, on Christmas eve, following another night of singing and drinking, he is suddenly struck by the error of his ways and goes home to his family for a tearful reunion. While cheaply and quickly made, reminiscent of a 1950s British B-movie, it features some superb music and thoroughly authentic scenes inside Fado Houses. It also reaffirms the Salazar propaganda of strong family ties underpinning both individual and societal behaviour.

By 1945, with the European war ended and Portugal poised to join the United Nations, the Fado's refurbished image was complete enough to allow the professional Fadista to become an acceptable public figure. A star that grew from, and was supported by, a system increasingly dedicated to entertainment was now a viable proposition. The Fado continued to be promoted as 'typically Portuguese' and, as an increasingly large number of foreign visitors passed through Lisbon for trade or tourist purposes, the Fado Houses rose to the occasion and became more and more commercially orientated. From this altered perception grew the career of the single most influential and important Fadista, Amália Rodrigues.

Amália Rodrigues

Born in Lisbon in 1920, her mother a vegetable stallholder, Amália spent the latter part of her teenage years attempting, without success, to gain a foothold in the theatre. By early 1940, however, she had earned a reputation as a remarkable Fadista, singing in the Solar De Alegria. João Reis, writing in the 1 March issue of

A Canção do Sul, which featured her photo on the cover, noted that her performances were drawing large and enthusiastic audiences. Almost a year later, in the same journal, he referred to her as a familiar figure on the Fado House circuit, praising her 'wonderful natural voice'.

The attention she received as a Fadista brought her to the notice of impresario António Macedo, who was staging a new revista, 'Ora Vai Tu!' at the Teatro Maria Vitoria. As a result Amália was given a relatively modest role in this show, followed a year later by a special appearance in Macedo's new revista 'Esera de Toiros' at the Teatro Varieadades. In this new production she sang three Fados and from then on appeared in every Macedo show until 1945. She had, in the meantime, travelled to Madrid in 1943 and Rio de Janeiro the following year. By 1945 she had gained sufficient experience to launch herself into an international career that would take both her and the Fado itself far beyond the borders of the Lusophone world.

On her second tour of Brazil, in 1945, Amália made a series of 78rpm records for the Rio-based 'Continental' label. Released first in Brazil, then imported directly into Portugal, and finally leased to Melodia for Portuguese distribution, they sold in huge quantities, greater than any Portuguese records had ever done. They deserved to – her music was a refreshing mix of the traditional and the innovative; going directly against the tide of increasingly homogeneous performance, the range and depth of her emotion both redefined and crystallized the sound of the Fado for the postwar years. Her remarkable voice immediately captured the public imagination.

With her reputation growing from strength to strength, she appeared in Armando Miranda's 1947 film 'Capas Negras', a cheerfully silly story of the relationship between the vivacious 'Maria De Lisboa' (Rodrigues) and a stuffy Coimbra University professor (Alberto Ribeiro). In the same year she starred in 'Fado, História D'uma Cantadeira', in which her meteoric rise to stardom was paralleled in the story of Ana Maria, the wife of a guitarra-maker whose remarkable singing voice brings her commercial success at the expense of her relationship with her husband and daughter. It was essentially the same plot as Farinha's 'O Muido da Bica', but Rodrigues's performance showed her to be as good an actress as a Fadista. A strong-featured and strikingly good-looking woman, by the time this film had been released, she was unquestionably the biggest Portuguese-speaking star since Carmen Miranda, with whom some, bizarrely, were beginning to compare her.

The leasing of her 'Continental' recordings to Melodia enabled Rádio Triunfo, who owned the label, to negotiate a recording contract with her. Throughout 1950 and 1951 they held three recording sessions in Lisbon, releasing fourteen 78rpm couplings, the first four with a somewhat turgid orchestral accompaniment, the last ten in the much more sympathetic company of guitarra and viola. By 1951, with two more films, an award from the Portuguese film industry for best new actress, appearances in Paris, London, Berlin, Rome, Dublin, Berne, Trieste, São Paulo, Mozambique and Angola behind her, Amália's contract with

Melodia records expired. On 27 September 1951, Valentim de Carvalho wrote to EMI at Hayes:

> Less than one year ago American Columbia tried to make arrangements with Amália for recording in Paris. It was arranged that Columbia would send a representative to Lisbon in April last to finalise everything, and arrange recordings in Paris. This person did not come.
>
> Now she has offers from Portuguese companies for recordings in Spanish, and they would pay her about £50 flat per record, and then a royalty of 6d. per record. She has had these offers before American Columbia came. The Americans would not pay her so much. Apart from American Columbia, French Polydor, French Decca, Columbia of Spain, Brazilian Continental and Portuguese Melodia have been trying to record her.
>
> The artist would prefer to make a contract with Columbia of UK, probably on a royalty of 5% if she could be guaranteed that the records would be published everywhere, including the U.S. and Brazil. The artists's repertoire is principally Portuguese, but she can also sing in French and Spanish. Is it possible for the company to consider making a direct contract with the artiste, and undertaking recordings in Paris or Lisbon, wherever she may be.[19]

EMI warmly agreed that it would be in the best interests of both themselves and Carvalho if Amália could be signed to a contract. One of their chief Artists and Recording (A&R) managers, Leonard Smith, was assigned to capture her for the company. On 14th November, he wrote to her at her home on Rua de S. Bernardo in Lisbon:

> On various visits to Paris I had hoped to meet you personally, but seem to have missed you each time. My company would very much like to make recordings with you with particular view for issue in Portugal, South and North America. I would like to suggest a contract with you on the following basis:-

Period	One year
Option	One year
Titles	A minimum of 8 per year
Royalty	5% of the retail price of the country of manufacture

> I sincerely hope that you will record for Columbia and such recordings could either be made in Paris or in London and if it is necessary for you to make a special visit at our request, then of course we would pay your travelling and hotel expenses.[20]

In the meantime EMI-Hayes wrote to their Rio branch, Industrias Elétricas e Musicales Fábrica Odeon SA, informing them of the potential recording session. They replied immediately and enthusiastically, suggesting a programme of songs that they felt she should record. Amália, having accepted the offer from EMI, left Lisbon on 25 February for Paris and then journeyed to Berne, Switzerland where Leonard Smith cabled her on the 14 March:

> HAVE APPLIED FOR LABOUR IMMIGRATION PERMIT FOR YOUR RECORDING STOP DO NOT TRAVEL UNTIL WE CABLE OK STOP[21]

At this time, the British Musicians' Union was operating a policy that excluded foreign musicians from working on British soil unless it could conclusively be proved that a British musician could not provide an adequate substitute. Because of this, many American jazz musicians, for instance, were excluded from playing in Britain until 1956 when a new agreement was reached. The Ministry of Labour would therefore not grant temporary work permits to foreign artists unless it could be assured by the Musicians' Union that a British musician was not going to be put out of work as a result. On the same day that he cabled Amália in Berne, Smith wrote to the Ministry:

> Further to my telephone conversation with you of this afternoon regarding the above mentioned artist, Amália Rodrigues, I am attaching the necessary application form for a permit.
>
> As I explained to you, it is impossible to secure this type of talent in this country, because the artist sings in Portuguese and is an individual specialist of her type.
>
> I wonder if, when the permit is ready, it will be troubling you too much if you could have somebody telephone me or my secretary so that I could send round to collect the permit in view of the urgency of the matter.[22]

Finally convinced, the Ministry issued a temporary permit and Amália, in the company of guitarrista Raúl Nery and viola player Santos Moreira, arrived in London a few days later. On Sunday, 23 March, and again on Thursday 27 March the three musicians made a total of 18 songs at EMI's Abbey Road studios in St John's Wood, London. Two of them were titles that the Rio office had suggested. On 31 March a clearly happy Leonard Smith sent C. H. Thomas, of the Overseas Department at Hayes, a memo:

> Confirming my conversation with you, I am pleased to tell you that we recorded 18 sides with Miss Rodrigues and her two guitarists, 16 are 10" and the other 2 are 12".
>
> The playbacks sound magnificent and I feel sure that we have some really big sellers.
>
> I am also happy to tell you that the artiste signed a period contract. She seemed very happy with the recordings and with the attention we gave her. I personally met her at the airport and got her tickets for theatres, etc.[23]

On the same day, he wrote to Valentim de Carvalho, essentially repeating what he had told Thomas and adding:

> As soon as test pressings are through I shall let you have them and if it is at all possible I might come to Lisbon to play them to you and Miss Rodrigues. I shall be very glad to make your acquaintance and to see your delightful country.[24]

Nery and Moreira received £72 each plus expenses for their work in London; Amália, receiving 5% royalties, got her first payment, of £33.3.11d. on 20 January 1953. At a retail price of 2/6d. this represented total sales of over 5000 copies of the four couplings issued by that time. When, in July of that year, EMI issued the one 12" coupling it had recorded, the monthly *Gramophone* magazine noted:

> Amália Rodrigues is reputed to be a supreme exponent of the characteristic 'Lisbon Fado'. After hearing 'Tudo Isto o Fado' (Columbia DLX-1) I call for more, and in doing so shall be surprised if I am not anticipating popular demand.[25]

On 18 March 1953, both parties, very satisfied with one another's performance, signed a contract for a further year.

Amália's career now began to grow internationally, with appearances in Mexico City, New York, Hollywood, Paris, Madrid, Rio de Janeiro, São Paulo,

Caracas and London between 1952 and 1955. Her association with EMI-Carvalho remained fruitful and, in 1955, she was among the first Portuguese artists to appear on LP record. That same year she starred in a successful revival of Júlio Dantes' 'A Severa' at the Teatro Monumental, and in three films, 'Os Amantes do Tejo', 'Primavera em Portugal' and 'Música de Sempre'. The first was a drama, the second a 20-minute travelogue for the tourist industry and the third a musical anthology that also included performances by Edith Piaf, Yma Sumac and the Argentinian Tango singer Libertad Lamarque.

From 1956 to 1960 Amália had appeared anually at the Olympia theatre in Paris. The 1960 concert, a *tour de force* of energy and emotion, was recorded live and issued within weeks on a 12" LP by EMI-Carvalho. The parent company at Hayes picked up the option to issue it in Britain, most of continental Europe, North and South America, Japan and South Africa, and it met with enormous success. Although already established as an international artist, the sales of this LP were large enough to further raise public awareness of her worldwide. At the start of the new decade, therefore, her reputation was consolidated and her future assured.

Amália's influence at home was felt in the shift towards an imitation of her style by a rising generation of women Fadistas. The sound now heard in many Fado Houses, on radio and record, was essentially the 'Amália' sound. This development had both a negative and positive impact upon the Fado. Because Amália's style was so intense, with its roots thoroughly planted in the old traditions, the goals of her imitators were at least authentic; at the same time few could achieve her emotional and technical levels, and the overall sound of the professional Fado was now increasingly homogeneous. This in turn led to expectations by a growing tourist industry for a recognizable sound to be offered to its clients. By the middle of the 1950s the Fado had settled into a style that was emblematic of a city increasingly geared for tourism. It was also dominated by professional women performers.

1960 to the present

With tourism playing an increasingly important role in the Portuguese economy, the Fado Houses entered a financial golden period at the dawn of the 1960s. Travel agents started to ask for brochures from the Fado Houses to entice the traveller with an image of a traditional Portugal easily accessible through the experience of taking a meal in a restaurant. Argentina Santos, who had opened her 'Perreirinha d'Alfama' establishment in 1950, now advertised through this new medium, describing her restaurant as 'The most typical and traditional pousada of the old Fado that exists in the heart of the Alfama.'[26]

Here, the foreign tourist could be fed with 'traditional' food, served in 'traditional' surroundings while enjoying 'traditional' Fado. Certainly, there was nothing essentially false about any of the things on offer. The Fadistas had simply repackaged themselves attractively enough to sell to an audience who wanted the quick and readily-available experience inherent in commercial tourism. Some Fado Houses extended the entertainment to include dance routines of a quasi-folkloric nature, with the audience encouraged to join in as the performance climaxed. This had almost nothing in common with the real experience of Portuguese rural dance, and was staged strictly for tourists.

However, original Fado styles persisted in bars and restaurants away from the tour guides' well-trodden paths. These were the places where working-class people still gathered for informal sessions; a tradition with a long history, unbroken to this day.

> There are places in the city which do not depend solely on Fado shows, but on a certain day of the week are transformed into meeting places for amateur Fadistas to get together, sing and be heard. They can be either bars and restaurants, which attract a larger audience on these nights, or recreational sports or cultural societies that use the Fado as a means of fund-raising for cultural purposes or their own upkeep.
>
> The sessions are long and the Fadistas perform in the order they arrive in, and alternate between the audience space and the singing area. The Fadistas themselves are the audience, making these sessions real occasions for communication. Each act is judged by the enthusiastic applause accorded to good performances; the styles, repertoire, voice quality and good co-ordination with the musicians are all discussed. According to the proprietor of one of these places, his bar is intended to be an 'atelier', where the Fado is innovated, experimented with and learned, thus filling the gap caused by the lack of schools teaching how to sing and play it. The most highly regarded performers see their reputations enhanced, while the novices can evaluate their talent and form social contacts.[27]

The *status quo* established during the 1950s and entrenched throughout the following decade was still operating when, in 1974, Portugal underwent the turmoil of political revolution. Opinions about the Fado, its role both in the past and the present, were as sharply divided in 1974 as they had been when the military regime took control 48 years earlier. The Fado itself had been used as a signal, nationwide, that the revolution was coming:

> From the 1960s there were big academic movements, like those in France, and it was then that Fado began to express difficulties with the regime. We had a very well known Fadista, Zeca Afonso, who sang a song that told of the vulture who came and ate everything, 'Vultures are coming and they are eating our bones and our souls', he was describing exploitation and oppression in a political way – repression of ideas, economic depression. So he used the traditional Fado and his skills to tell a metaphoric story that was well understood, and that people could sing. In the night of the revolution, the song gave the sign to come to invade Lisbon.[28]

This use of the Fado for revolutionary purposes polarized opinion along political lines. The Salazarians not only resented the left wing for bringing an almost 50 year regime to a close, they also bristled at the use of the Fado as a call to arms. For their part, the revolutionaries rejected much traditional and commercial Fado, claiming it to be tainted by Salazarianism:

> The traditional Fado had become considered reactionary, and it stayed in the right-wing where they held closed parties and sang the old Fado. It was not possible, in that social context, to love it, or teach it to your children.[29]

The two-year period following the revolution was one of chaos and almost perpetual revolution. The new government divested Portugal of the old colonial territories of East Timor, Mozambique and Angola, a decision which resulted in thousands of destitute and often embittered refugees arriving in Portugal. Continuing political upheaval, sparked by the struggle for power between the Movimento das Forças Armadas (MFA), the Portuguese Communist Party (PCP) and the Socialist Party resulted in several abrupt changes of government. By 1975, following a further abortive coup by the army, Mário Soares's Socialist Party gained enough support to form a relatively stable government that lasted until 1980, when the newly formed Democratic Alliance, a merged group of rightist parties, took control. Portuguese society survived this extraordinary six-year trauma to emerge, at the dawn of the 1980s, as a relatively stable and certainly much liberalized society.

The challenges presented to the Fado by a post-revolutionary society entering a new decade prompted a number of changes. The economic necessity of promoting the tourist trade ensured that the activities of the Fado Houses needed to continue uninterrupted, and the semi-private amateur Fado sessions, regardless of the political leanings of the participants, proceeded unabated. However, beginning around 1981, the term 'Fado Vadio' (Disreputable Fado) began to be used to describe a new type of musical experience. Sixty or more years previously, in a past dim enough that few had recollection of it, the term was used by aristocrats and theatre-goers to describe what went on in the rough-and-tumble taverns of the working classes. Now, the term was being re-employed to describe and promote a specific kind of restaurant where an ambience of rough and unruly behaviour was actively promoted. Fadistas were 'planted' in the audience and then came forward to sing when a request was made for an amateur volunteer to take a turn. This served as an antidote to the increasingly tired formula offered by the established Fado Houses, and was aimed at the new, supposedly more streetwise, generation of tourists, people who wanted to experience a foreign country 'in the raw' rather than through the rose-tinted spectacles offered to them by a conservative tourist industry. Undeniably opportunistic in concept, and arguably deceptive in practice, Fado Vadio nevertheless offered a good evening's entertainment, especially if the participants could be encouraged to end the proceedings with a fiery argument leading to a display of near-violence. Their success drew customers away from the older style of Fado House, many of which closed during the eighties. Closer to the spirit of tradition, however, was the existence of a few genuine Fado Houses, such as those that could be found in the Alfama, the Bica district or tucked away in the Bairro Alto, just a few steps away from the gaudy frontages of the commercial establishments.

*   *   *

In 1987, I spent a long period in Lisbon, attempting to understand something about the music that I had so recently encountered and become enamoured with.

On the day following my arrival, I met a lottery-ticket salesman on the street in the Roçio; his name was Júlio Martins, and he was also a self-published poet. After some cross-conversation in broken English and Portuguese, I finally convinced him that I wanted to see 'the real Fado', not any of the tourist versions, and he directed me to the Taverna do Barata on Rua dos Mouros, just off the Rua Rosa in the Bairro Alto. The name was a pun, for Barata means both 'cheap' and 'cockroach' in Portuguese.

Unusually for a Fado House, the sessions started at 6pm and ran only for three hours. Júlio advised me to arrive at least half an hour early. Even with instructions, it took some finding; there was nothing whatever to indicate that number 10 Rua dos Mouros was a Fado House. I stood outside a little uneasily in the muggy October evening, trying to decide which of two identical but unmarked doors to go through. I didn't want to burst uninvited into someone's living room. When I finally chose a door and entered, I knew I had found the right place. Bathed in a low yellow light, the Taverna do Barata was divided into two areas; in the front, a small square arena with a bar to the left and a massive old American refrigerator opposite, almost buried beneath stacked chairs and soft drinks crates. Perched on top was a portable television blaring the evening news. In front of me, and behind a beaded curtain, lay a narrow room about fifteen feet in length. Along the right-hand wall were ranged two benches, in front of which were set a pair of tables covered in oilcloth. Opposite them, and separated by perhaps only eighteen inches, was a random collection of chairs and upended drinks crates. A tattered and stained poster of Amália Rodrigues was pinned up on the door that led out from this room to a small kitchen. At one table sat a neat, grey-suited man eating a fish supper. I took a seat at the empty table, cradling a glass of wine, and nodded to him. His name was Jorges Neves, and his English was much better than my Portuguese. When he realized that I was not lost, but had actually spent time and energy finding the place, he launched into his version of Fado history, one which denounced anything outside of Lisbon and had its roots firmly planted in the maritime experience. He sang as much as he spoke, launching into brief acapella examples of the old styles and the differences between them. At 6.00pm he left, saying he would meet me the next evening. I never saw him again. Moments later two men arrived in the front of the taverna, exchanged greetings with the old couple who ran it and took delivery of the house instruments, a guitarra and a viola, that were kept in a cupboard to the right of the bar. I watched them pass me and take up seats at the far table that Jorges had just vacated. They ignored my presence at first and involved themselves in tuning their instruments. Then they turned their attention to me and we all introduced ourselves. The guitarra player was a stocky, muscular, bespectacled man with thinning hair. The viola player was a shorter, thinner man with a placid smile and receding crown. Both were in their sixties and smartly dressed. Avelino Vicente, the guitarra player, had been a boxer in his youth, travelling to the United States to compete in matches in New York, Boston and Chicago during the 1940s. He was very talkative and animated. His partner Adelino Inácio remained pleasantly aloof and enigmatic, as he would continue to do. They ran roughly through a few instrumentals, clearly anticipating the arrival of someone to accompany.

On that first night, a Monday, only a few men struggled in to listen and sing. Among them was a coach driver named José Reis. A warm and friendly barrel of a man whose hard life showed clearly in his face, he turned from talking to me to singing a Fado as naturally as he would have turned to another friend to make a comment. It was the first time I had heard a Fado sung live at close range, and suddenly all that I had read about this music simultaneously made sense and yet seemed wholly inadequate.

In successive evenings at the Taverna Barata, I met and listened to many other amateur Fadistas. Mario Augusto was in his mid-thirties, a handsome man who a decade earlier had tried and failed to turn professional. He worked as a tram engineer, wrote new songs constantly and possessed a beautiful voice. Joaquim Pessoa was in his mid-eighties – 'He's crazy', said José – a tall, lean, weathered man in a black felt hat with animated smoking habits and a cracked singing voice that brought deep respect from his peers. Mario Alves, who worked for the Agfa Film company, brought an operatic tenor voice to the proceedings and had to be dissuaded from breaking into arias from *Rigoletto*. Every time he tried, he was booed and hissed by an audience with an indulgent smile in its eyes. There were others whose names I never knew, who appeared suddenly and then melted away again. One was a woman, no more than forty, but weathered, harassed and toothless. She stood up to sing a Fado about the beating she had taken just a few hours earlier from her partner; the bruises on her face revealing themselves in the yellow light as she moved. An astringent man of about 85, dressed in old but expensive clothes, with a diamond tie-pin, sang a Fado about imminent death. A young man concealing a withered arm, an air of quiet desperation on his face, sang 'Guitarras de Lisboa' with a voice that seemed breathless and almost spent. On busy nights the room became impossibly choked, people jostling each other for strategic positions, crowding so close that they shared the exhaled smoke and extruded sweat.

It was in these circumstances that I learned the basic rules of a Fado House. People sang in the order in which they arrived, an elected tallyman keeping a list and indicating by hand signals who would be next. No-one sang more than three songs, and each song was roughly three minutes long. Avelino and Adelino took no instrumental solos, they simply accompanied. Each turn, therefore, lasted approximately ten minutes and no noise whatsoever was tolerated while singing was in progress. The hubbub that erupted between each song faded away as the guitarra began an introduction and residual conversation was halted by a collective 'ssshhh' issuing from the audience. Each song was accorded deep and rapt attention, watched and felt as well as heard, a total experience that involved everyone in the room. A Fado's climax is always indicated by the singer's voice rising to a crescendo of volume and emotion, as if the best were held back until the end. In the same second that the final note is uttered, a good performance will elicit a wave of applause, cheering, foot stamping and whistling. For especially good performances the appelation 'Fadista', shouted loudly and pronounced 'FAAAAADEEEEESHTAAA', will be used. The singer will generally nod, eyes closed, in acknowledgement. If, on the other hand, the audience judges the performance too poor to be allowed to continue, the singer will be rudely halted, often in mid-song, and told in very clear terms that they are rubbish. On the two occasions that I witnessed this, fierce debate erupted, involving loud and coarse exchanges of views, saliva and aggressive body language, but no real violence.

It was here also that I first encountered the 'desafio'. Two singers, in this case of opposite sex, engage in a verbal duel, insulting one another in turn, making ribald comments about each other's families, threatening to expose foibles in one another that they hint at knowledge of. José Reis and Suzette Carvalho sang this on the second Friday night session that I attended. At first, so far as I was concerned, José was singing a solo Fado, but after the initial verse I was surprised to hear Suzette answering him from the table next to me. She moved as she sang, joining José in the cramped space in front of the tables where the desafio continued in an animated fashion. The essence of this particular song was a couple's mutual distaste for their partner's family.

> You're family's vulgar, if I'd known how bad they were I'd have dumped you at the start, you farting pig.
>
> You can talk, you fat old bag! Your no-good brother does nothing but sponge off us.
>
> At least he's honest; I can't say the same for your father.
>
> You want to talk about criminals? He's a saint compared to your lot. The jail's full of your family, you slag.
>
> That's dangerous talk; you'll get a bottle over your head if you're not careful, you lying bastard.

At this point, José and Suzette are waving empty bottles at each other, laughing as they continue to sling insults in song; the audience is egging them on, taking sides, shouting comments and laughing with them. A desafio, unlike a Fado, is not listened to in hushed tones; far from it, it's an opportunity to join in the fun, be as rowdy as possible. Those who cannot or will not sing will join in the free-for-all of a desafio. The song ends when inspiration deserts one or the other, and they cannot reply. On this occasion Suzette won, and she and José collapsed into each other's arms howling with laughter, as the room exploded into applause and cheers.

The other occasion on which audience participation is allowable is when someone sings a 'Fado Falar'. It translates literally as 'Talking Fado', and is a sung narrative with a chorus that the audience may participate in. Mario Augusto loved to sing Fado Falar, and was constantly inventing new ones, based on old familiar tunes that the audience would recognize. If the words of the chorus escaped some audience members, it was perfectly acceptable to hum along, and Mario could always get the room humming. The original Fado Falar, popular in the 19th century, was often a long, extemporized narrative about a specific and (often) true event; a sensational crime, or some ongoing social trend. Mario sang about the life of a fireman, or the events of the 1974 revolution; his chorus was always catchy and familiar, his comments often funny and biting. When he sang, Mario became animated, more alive, and very attractive. When he stopped, he seemed to retreat back inside himself, becoming the shy man that the outside world ignored on a daily basis.

Throughout my first two weeks visiting the Taverna do Barata, an elderly man had sat by himself in the far corner, speaking to no-one, nodding only occasionally to a few specific people. He drank little, nursing his beer and often cradling his head in his hands. He looked terribly depressed. José told me he was very old, perhaps ninety or more, and had lived in the Bairro Alto all his life. He had been a Fadista in the old days, but didn't sing anymore, because he believed his voice had lost its power. He just came and listened.

One evening he produced a crumpled piece of paper which, after a few moments of hesitation, he handed to Adelino. It was a list of songs, and Adelino conferred with Avelino then with the old man, in hoarse and urgent whispers. The guitarra played a familiar introduction and, to the astonishment of everyone, the old man rose to sing a 'Fado Velho' – an old Fado. His voice was surprisingly strong; he sang with great attack, punctuating his delivery with animated hand gestures, staring wildly around the room as he performed. His phrasing and delivery seemed archaic, I had heard nothing like it before, either in the tavern or on the few records I then possessed. With hindsight I know that he was singing the way men sang in the taverns during the early part of the century, but that evening he presented me with a wholly new experience. I was aware, I think, of how rare his style was, and had this confirmed later by Mario who, as surprised as I was, told me he'd not heard anything like it for years.

I attended every session at the Taverna Barata for a number of weeks; the singers became familiar with my presence and I made many friends. The price of the drinks dropped sharply; I was now paying the same as the regulars. On one Tuesday evening I was introduced by José to Vicente de Camara. The deference in José's voice alerted me to the importance of this character. Vicente was a professional Fadista and, moreover, a legendary figure. Now a stocky and well-preserved man with silver hair and a quiet smile, Vicente had started to sing Fados while he was in his teens, learning from an uncle, João do Carmo de Noronha, who had made records in 1926. Vicente had won a Fado contest when he was 20 and started to appear in Fado Houses towards the middle of the 1940s, then secured a contract to perform regularly on Emissora Nacional, the national radio station. A recording session with EMI-Carvalho followed and by 1951 he was a firmly established star. His presence in the Taverna Barata created an extraordinary atmosphere of respect and awe. People moved more quietly, talked in lower tones, glancing up to assure themselves that he really was who they thought. He didn't sing, he listened and applauded; when the session ended at 9.00pm he shook everyone's hand and then left. His behaviour was evidence of a saying I'd heard earlier in my trip: that the listener is just as much a Fadista as the singer.

1.   Lisbon, undated postcard

2.   A blind Fadista, undated engraving, artist unknown

3.   A Fado in the street, photograph by Rodney Gallop, *c.* 1930

4.   *The Fadistas*, engraving by Rafael Bordalo Pinheiro, 1783

Columbia

APRESENTA

NOVOS DISCOS PORTUGUESES

EDITADOS PELOS

Est. VALENTIM DE CARVALHO

LISBOA — Rua Nova do Almada, 95-99

PORTO — Rua de Santo António, 176

(Vadeca Lda. Agentes)

5. Columbia record catalogue, 1944

6.   Madalena de Mello, 1929

DISCOS DE GUITARRA

ARMANDINHO (Guitarra) com acomp. de viola
por Georgino de Souza

EQ 152 (Fado em lá maior — *Armandinho.*
       (Fado Peniche — *Armandinho.*

EQ 153 (Fado Alexandrino — *Armandinho.*
       (Fado Armandinho.

EQ 166 (Fados do Estoril — *Armandinho.*
       (Fado em mi menor — *Armandinho.*

EQ 189 (Magioli — *Magioli.*
       (Fado Conde Anadia — *Conde Anadia.*

EQ 197 (Fado Bacalhau — *Armandinho.*
       (Marcha em ré maior — *Armandinho.*

EQ 204 (Variações em ré menor — *A. Freire-*
       (*Petroline.*
       (Fado Fernandinha — *A. Freire.*

7.   Armandinho, undated HMV publicity postcard

MARIA SILVA (Soprano)
com acomp. de guitarra e viola

EQ 144 (Fado Franklin.
       (Fado corrido.

EQ 145 (Fado-Tango.
       (Fado Alice.

EQ 163 (Fado da Moda.
       (Fado da Mouraria.

EQ 186 (Fado da Paixão.
       (Fado dos dois tons.

8.   Maria Silva, undated HMV publicity postcard

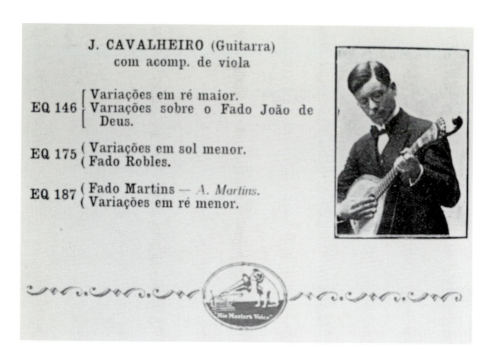

9. J. Cavalheiro, undated HMV publicity postcard

10. Adelina Fernandes, 1927

11.   Edmundo de Bettencourt, undated

12.   Artur Paredes, 1928

13. Ricardo Lemos's premises in Porto, undated

14. J. Castello Branco advertisement, 1910, from *Illustração Portuguesa*

15. Maria Severa, undated drawing

16. Amália Rodrigues and Virgilio Teixeira, 1947, from *Amália: uma biografia por Vítor Pavão dos Santos*, Contexto editora, 1987

17.   Amália Rodrigues playing a guitarra, 1953, from *Amália: uma biografia por Vítor Pavão dos Santos*, Contexto editora, 1987

18.   Carlos Zell, 1995

19. Mafalda Arnauth, 1995

My experiences in the Taverna Barata and other, more accessible, Fado houses during that first trip paralleled those of Lawton McCaul and Rodney Gallop, whose accounts I was already familiar with. From these I knew that at the heart of Fado's history was continuum rather than revival, and that tourist-Fado and other attempts to place the music in a more populist context were essentially ephemeral, did not damage the core of the music, but merely obscured it. As recently as 1995 I had this demonstrated to me by the activities of three Fadistas, Argentina Santos, Carlos Zel and the young Mafalda Arnouth. They are by no means the only important Fadistas currently singing, but their ages, styles and experiences are representative of the state of the music as the millennium approaches.

I first encountered them briefly in Lisbon in the spring of 1995. I had been introduced to Argentina at her restaurant, the Perririnha d'Alfama, just after she had finished singing, but she had no time then for extended conversation. I met Carlos Zel the same night, in another Fado House. It was late, there were few customers and the atmosphere was more relaxed. Carlos performed, standing behind his accompanists, in an ancient, low-ceilinged and flagstoned cellar bar that echoed to his voice. Mafalda had preceded him, but I arrived just as she was singing her last song.

All three appeared at the Queen Elizabeth Hall in London during September of the same year. Argentina is the oldest; born Maria Argentina Pinto dos Santos, in the Mouraria in 1926, she is of the same generation as Amália Rodrigues and is perhaps the best traditional female singer in Lisbon today. Her recording career started in 1952, with 78rpm releases on the Estoril label, and her style is closer to the cafes of the 1920s than any other era. Now in her seventies she remains vibrant, strong and very active. Carlos, a recording artist since the 1970s with a number of local hit records behind him, also sings the traditional Fado, and his warm, clear tenor delivery is in the mainstream of the Lisbon male tradition. Mafalda, born in 1975, had only been singing for three years when she appeared in London.

> I was at Lisbon University in 1992 and I heard a tape by Amália Rodrigues and I said 'I can do that'. People encouraged me and that's how it all started. I sung at the University, then around Lisbon, then I got to go to Luxembourg, but they didn't like the Portuguese there very much. Then I sang in Paris. That was a success and now I'm excited to come here and sing, especially with Carlos and Argentina, I learn so much from them.[30]

Together, Argentina, Carlos and Mafalda represent three generations of traditional Fado singing. That tradition can still be experienced nightly in Lisbon and, as one Fadista said to me on my first trip:

> The Fado has always been here, since Severa's time. Think about this; every night for all this century, there's been Fado singing in this town. It's in the air, in the streets, it's everywhere. They were singing Fado the night I was born and they'll sing it the night I die.'[31]

Notes

1. Rodney Gallop (1936), *Portugal – A Book of Folkways*, Cambridge: CUP.
2. Joaquim Pais de Brito (1994), *Voices and Shadows* (1994), Lisbon: Electra.
3. Gordon, Jan & Cora (1934), *Portuguese Somersault*, London: George Harrap & Co.
4. Rodney Gallop (1936), *Portugal – A Book of Folkways*, Cambridge: CUP.
5. Uncredited transcript of a 1935 BBC radio broadcast in the Gallop collection.
6. GBDP to Hayes, 2.7.29/EMI Archives.
7. Hayes to Victor, Brazil 2.8.29/EMI Archives.
8. A Canção do Sul, 1.2.32.
9. Rodney Gallop (1936), *Portugal – A Book of Folkways*, Cambridge: CUP.
10. Lawton McCaul (1931), *Portugal for Two*, NYC: Dodd, Mead & Co.
11. Berta Cardosa interview in *Voices and Shadows* (1994), Lisbon: Electra.
12. Chevas poster, 1930 in *Voices and Shadows*, op. cit.
13. Gallop (1931), *The Gramophone*, October.
14. Retiro de Severa advt, *Voices and Shadows*, op. cit.
15. A Canção do Sul, 1.11.38.
16. Salwa El-Shawan Castelo-Branco, *Voices and Shadows*, op. cit.
17. Eduardo Sucena (1992), *Lisboa, O fado e os Fadistas*, Lisbon: Vega Press.
18. *Diario de Noticias*, 1937.
19. EMI-Hayes to Carvalho, 27.9.51/EMI Archives.
20. Leonard Smith to Amália Rodrigues, 14.2.52/EMI Archives.
21. Ibid.
22. Leonard Smith to the Ministry of Labour, 14.2.52/EMI Archives.
23. Leonard Smith to C. H. Thomas, 31.3.52/EMI Archives.
24. Leonard Smith to Valentim de Carvalho, 31.3.52/EMI Archives.
25. *The Gramophone*, July 1953.
26. Brochure for the 'Perrinha d' Alfama', c. 1960.
27. Alexandre Klein, *Voices and Shadows*, op. cit.
28. Prof. Salwa El-Shawan Castelo-Branco in conversation with the author, Lisbon, November 1987.
29. Alexandre Klein, *Voices and Shadows*, op. cit.
30. Mafalda Arnouth in conversation with the author, London, October 1995.
31. José Reis in conversation with the author, Lisbon, October 1987.

4 Coimbra and Porto

There is a quality peculiar to university towns which other ancient cities do not share. It is as though, in the flower of their age, they had stumbled upon the secret of eternal youth. But university cities have succeeded in harnessing the vigour of youth to the wisdom of maturity. They are the slowly formed product of the vitality, the enthusiasms, the illusions of each succeeding generation, superimposed upon the humanism and philosophy of those that have gone before.

In Coimbra one is intensely aware of this spirit. It is the third city in Portugal, was once the capital, and is still the seat of the second-oldest university in Europe. White houses spilt over a hill above the river Mondego impart to it an air of youthful charm and freshness. Both materially and spiritually it is dominated by the tall clock tower of the university, a shining beacon to which the eyes of the city seem eternally to be lifted.

In the narrow, winding streets one is constantly meeting bare-headed students, in black frock coats and flowing gowns, carrying satchels tied with ribbons in the different colours of the faculties; yellow for medicine, red for law, blue for letters and so forth. University life, here, is in some ways similar to and in other ways different from our own. An elaborate code of traditions and gradually earned privileges make the life of the caloiro (freshman) scarcely worth living. The students live in hostels and indulge in 'rags' culminating in the Queima das Fitas, when, on the conclusion of their fourth year, the quartanistas make a public bonfire of their ribbons. Some days after this ceremony the Republica dos Grilos, painted with two enormous cockroaches and the mysterious inscription 'Ab Urbe Ondita A.D. 70' was still festively hung with a guy, a couple of wicker chairs, a bath, a guitar and a variety of household utensils, some of the most intimate nature. This building belonged at one time to the professors, but some thirty years ago the students, acting on a sudden, glorious inspiration, ejected them, and, installing themselves in their place, have never since been dislodged. Hero-worship at Coimbra is not dependent upon athletic prowess, but is bestowed upon those who sound most insistently the 'romantic' note, in song, poetry and extravagant actions.[1]

It was students such as these who, as the nineteenth century ended and the twentieth century began, took the ingredients of the Fado and, much to the disgust of Lisbon purists, moulded their own version of it. The Coimbra Fado, while retaining the bare essentials of form and instrumentation, turned the philosophy of the music around, altered its tone and approach, and produced a deeply romanticized vocal music that was the lyrical and spiritual antithesis of the Lisbon style. They sang not of hard times or lost love but of student life and philosophy, the beauty of Coimbra and the pain of being a sensitive artist in a philistine world.

45

The Coimbra students consciously drew lines between the two styles of Fado, and in doing so, challenged Lisbon with an 'extravagant action'.

Always an insightful observer of Portuguese culture, Rodney Gallop defined the Coimbra Fado as 'The song of those who still retain and cherish their illusions, not of those who have irretrievably lost them'.[2] His contextual descriptions of the genre, as he found it in the early 1930s, are still among the most vivid of all Fadocentric writing:

> At Coimbra the Fado has a very different character. Here it is no longer the song of the common people. It has become the property of the students who wander along the banks of the (river) Mondego, among the poplars of the Choupal, dreamily singing to their silvery guitars. Their clear, warm tenor voices give the song a character that is more refined, more sentimental, in a word, more aristocratic. At Coimbra the Fado seems divorced from everyday realities and cares, to be over-spiritualised, and to express a vague romantic yearning which is in keeping with the atmosphere of the ancient university city.[3]
>
> On full moonlight nights you may see the students in their black gowns wandering through the dim white streets and hear them singing the haunting strains of the Fado Chorado.[4]
>
> Once, at about two in the morning, I was awakened by the thrumming of a guitar in the street below. The terraced city shone palely in the light of the moon. In a deep shadow on the opposite side of the street four or five students were leaning against a wall looking up at a window. Presently, one of them began to sing in a warm tenor voice one of the old Fados de Coimbra, full of melancholy yearning. To me, as doubtless to others, music is often the golden key which, opening the doors of sensations, leads to apprehension of the secret things which lie at the hearts of places and of those who dwell in them. So it was with Coimbra. That song, floating upwards through the night, revealed the spirit of Coimbra as only its sons know and love it.[5]

Responsibility for popularizing the Coimbra vocal style is generally attributed to Augusto Hilario, a student who, according to the myths of the songs sung in his honour, brought the Lisbon Fado with him to university and reshaped it in the way Rodney Gallop describes, creating disciples of the new style as he did so. Hilario died in 1904, age 32, leaving little evidence of his existence. There are no photos, no musical examples or substantive biographical details; rumours of a cylinder recording persist but it remains undiscovered; his guitarra has survived, but sits silent in a museum. All that is really known about him is that he inspired his fellow students to sing in a new and radical way during the early 1890s. That there may have been earlier practitioners than Hilario, or at least contemporaries, seems entirely probable but remains unprovable. It is doubtful that Hilario developed the style single-handedly, and it further seems unlikely that he created it in a vacuum. The most plausible scenario is that he was part of a small coterie of practising musicians, the rest of whom have slipped from collective memory. Hilario's influence, however, as much spiritual as musical, permeated Coimbra at the turn of the century and one disciple, Manasses de Lacerda (b. 27 September 1885), did leave a legacy of early gramophone records. This included two versions of 'Fado Hilario', one for the German Beka company and a second for the English Gramophone Company, both recorded in Porto in 1905, after he had left

Coimbra. He was a high school, rather than a university, student and his academic abilities were apparently too poor to allow him to graduate. He therefore left Coimbra after his seventh year of high school and took up residence in Porto, although why he chose to settle there remains unclear. His style, declamatory and somewhat distant, is married by the limited recording techniques of the day and the unsympathetic piano accompaniment. Our ability to judge his worth must, therefore, be tempered by these circumstances.

Nevertheless, what can be gathered from Lacerda's recordings, of which 23 survive, is that the Fado he sang was (at least) a Fado in transition. It bore some resemblance to the contemporary Lisbon Fado, but had a more dramatic air to it, almost as if Lacerda were attempting to reproduce the Italian bel-canto style within a Lusophone framework. Whether anyone in Coimbra was either following Lacerda's lead or practising the full-blown romantic style that appeared on record a quarter of a century later is uncertain, but by 1914 the emerging Coimbra style had asserted itself within the closed society in which it operated and was enthusiastically embraced by both students and – often – their professors. It was seen as a badge, an emblem, worn as proudly as the colours that Gallop describes. To be an aficionado was de rigueur; to be a singer or a guitarrista was to achieve a status within the community that would often outshine academic success.

Menano and the 'Golden Era' of the Coimbra Fado

In 1914, António Paulo Menano entered Coimbra to study medicine. He was just 19 years old, and from a middle-class family in Fornos de Alodres, some 150 miles south-west of Coimbra. By 1919 Menano was involved in the organization of large festivals of Fado in Coimbra, had joined the Orfeão Acadêmico, a traditional Coimbran choral group, and with them had travelled throughout Portugal, Spain, France and Brazil. Despite his extra-curricular activities, Menano graduated as a doctor of medicine in 1923 and went home to set up his own surgery. His fame as a singer and songwriter, however, ensured that he would not slip into obscurity. That same year he appeared at the Coliseão de Recreios in Lisbon accompanied by guitarrista Artur Paredes and viola player José dos Santos. The following year he achieved notoriety when his singing provoked violently negative audience reaction at the same venue. This event adds weight to remarks that Rodney Gallop made:

> Dr. Menano's Fados are a bone of contention in Portugal. He composes many of them himself, and some say that he has departed too far from the genuine tradition. Others maintain that he sings Fados as no other has ever sung them before. His are certainly among the elite, and Fado de Sa Velha is one of the loveliest that I know.[6]

Menano also sang in Paris that year, although to apparently greater appreciation than in his home country. During 1925 he also returned to Brazil, not as a member of the Orfeão, but in his own right as a leading practitioner of the Coimbra style, and in the company of other celebrated Fadistas.

The style being forged in Coimbra was centred around Menano and another remarkably talented character, Dr Edmundo Alberto de Bettencourt. De Bettencourt was born in Funchal, on the island of Madeira, on 7 August 1899 and came to Coimbra in 1918 to study law. His talent for music was greater by far than his talent for law and, although he was referred to on record labels and in catalogues as 'Doctor', he never graduated. 'The purest and most crystalline scream a human throat can give' said Dr Carlos Figueiredo of de Bettencourt's singing. De Bettencourt gave regular evening concerts in Coimbra for the first half of the 1920s, toured Spain in 1923, Brazil in 1925 with Menano and others, and quickly achieved an almost mythical status among students.

Disciples of these two major figures included the Brazilian mathematics student Dr Lucas Rodrigues Junot, who as a 20-year-old joined the School of Science at Coimbra on 31 October 1922; José Paradella de Oliveira (1904–1970), who joined the School of Medicine in the autumn of 1924, and Armando Goes, another medical student who arrived at probably the same time as de Oliveira. There were others also, the details of whose lives are now lost but who nevertheless contributed to the recorded legacy that, in the brief but intense period from 1924 to 1931, secured and defined the Coimbra style for the future generations who would come to regard it as the 'Golden Era'.

The first singer since Lacerda to record, in about 1924, was Carvalho de Oliveira. Nothing is known of him, but his one recording session, for the French Pathé company, is pure Coimbra Fado. His work lay in isolation until the baritone Dr António Batoque recorded for Valentim de Carvalho, the Columbia agent, in August 1926. From then on the records were issued more regularly. In May 1927 Grand Bazaar do Porto held a lengthy session in Lisbon in conjunction with the Gramophone Company that included Paradella de Oliveira, Armando Goes and José Dias, all of whom were firmly under Menano's influence. Among other things, de Oliveira recorded 'Fado de Se Velha', 'O Meu Menino' and 'Fado De Santa Clara', while Goes sang 'Fado Espanhol', and Dias chose 'Fado Patrioco', all Menano compositions. In June the company issued its first printed catalogue of Portuguese Fados, carrying a logo of a stylized Coimbra Fadista and containing photos of all three singers, clearly taken outside the main university building in Coimbra.

At about the same time, Dr Menano went to Paris to record for the German-owned Odeon label. In the company of guitarrista Augusto Da Silva Louro and viola player Flávio Rodrigues, he recorded 34 titles, and while there the trio participated in a successful concert that included Pablo Casals and Tito Schipa, the earliest evidence we have of Fado appearing outside the Lusophone world with any measurable degree of success.

Menano's recording career continued in the spring of the following year with a Lisbon session that produced 20 sides, again accompanied by Louro and Rodrigues. In December he was in Odeon's Studio Three in Berlin with João Fernandes and Mário Marques, essentially Lisbon musicians, to record a further 45 songs. Menano's final recording session took place in early 1930 in Madrid.

He went there with a group of Lisbon singers and, as well as recording solo, took part in some remarkable duets with Ercília Costa and Joaquim Campos – unique in Portuguese recording history – that brought the singing styles of the two Fados together; an act that was almost bound to have caused furore in both Lisbon and Coimbra.

In 1928 Edmundo de Bettencourt travelled to Lisbon to record for the Gramophone Company's arch-rival Columbia. In February of that year, in a dusty upper room of Valentim de Carvalho's huge and rambling establishment on Rua Nova de Almada, de Bettencourt, accompanied by guitarristas Artur Paredes and Albano de Noronho and viola player Mário de Fonseca, recorded ten songs that Valentim de Carvalho quickly issued in a separate, prestigious and more expensive series. The de Bettencourt recordings cost 30 escudos, two and a half escudos more than a regular 10" record. In December of the following year he returned with Paredes, Fonseca and guitarrista Afonso de Sousa to record a further ten songs, the last of which was not secured until early January 1930. These records remained in catalogue until 1953, and de Bettencourt accrued royalties from them until their deletion. Specific sales figures appear not to have survived, but a 1939 EMI statement lists de Bettencourt pressings entirely separately, and it is interesting to note that the wholesale price for his recordings is no different from a regular pressing, leading to the conclusion that the two and a half escudos extra represented de Bettencourt's negotiated 8% royalty.

De Bettencourt's repertoire was a synthesis of Fado and traditional Portuguese folk-music remoulded into an academic framework. Contemporaries observed:

> Edmundo de Bettencourt was the greatest Fado singer of all times. He marked an era, he was decisive for improving Coimbra taste, having been above all a great poet.[7]

and, speaking of his arrangements of traditional folk tunes;

> He brought to Coimbra Fado the folk tunes that, from several regions of Continental Portugal, Madeira and the Acores converged to the University through students from all over the country and which therefore became an enriching patrimony of the Fados and ballads he left us, in perfect assimilation between the rustic and urban musical expressions.[8]

De Bettencourt's influence is still heard today in contemporary Coimbra playing. His collection of Fados, although not as extensive as those of Menano, remains an important ingredient of Coimbra repertoire, but perhaps more significantly he widened the appreciation of interpretive readings of rural folk music and fostered their acceptance. His recording of 'Canção da Beira Baixa', as well as being a *tour de force* of open-throated singing in a near bel-canto style, opened the doors, for the generations that followed, to continue the tradition of folkloric interpretation. He is still held in as much awe today as he was during his lifetime.

João Gaspar Simões remarked that after

> his glorious journey to Columbia records, he completely forgot the university existed. He bought a gramophone, acquired a photographic camera and didn't give another thought about his studies.[9]

De Bettencourt relocated to Lisbon and lived quietly until his death on 1 February 1973.

Meanwhile Menano disappeared for a number of years. Periodically he would resurface in Coimbra, stay awhile, visit old friends and then vanish again. No-one knew where; the rumours were that he was somewhere in the colonies but none knew for sure. Years later a poem by the Dutch writer J.J. Slauerhoff (1898–1936) was discovered that shed some light on the matter:

Compagnie de Mozambique

To the Compagnie de Mozambique
Belongs Beira
And the land behind it
And Manga too
And the blacks that work there
And the shrubs in the flower beds
All of it belongs
To the Compagnie de Mozambique

Also the animals that live here
Not only the limping oxes
With their tsetses*
Hovering birds and invisible insects too

It gets boring
To name it all
But what can you do
If you're waiting for a bus (of the Compagnie too)
That's not coming

Listening to the reed warbler
That with his straight two tone song
Is right in the middle
Between cricket and nightingale;

António Menano too
The famous Fado singer
At whose dark muffled voice
All women cry and faint
Who lifted the sorrow of Portugal
Menano too
Belongs to the Compagnie de Mozambique

Eight miles further on
He works at a plantation;
Rich he became for everyone wanted to hear him
Poor he became because he gambled and he lost
And of course he speculated in shares
Of the Compagnie de Mozambique

*Tsetse: a disease-carrying airborn insect

Now he is linked for seven years
There as a plantation surgeon
Giving injections and deciding
If a black who made a mistake
Is strong enough for the beating.

For the rules are severe but humane
At the Compagnie de Mozambique

Don't we bring together the bail
That he sings of sad blissfullness?
No. Menano, too drunk himself
Hoarse through whiskey that,
Imported at a lower rate
Is served to the employees
Of the Compagnie de Mozambique.[10]

By the early 1950s Menano was back in Coimbra, living in quarters opposite the old convent of St. Theresa. Despite absence in a far-flung colony and a complete lack of new recordings, his status remained undiminished. It had been over thirty years since he was booed offstage, and now Lisbon seemed ready to forgive him:

> The dawn recital he gave in the auditorium of Lisbon's Institute of Agronomy [in 1958] is still remembered. Menano was due to begin at midnight but only arrived at around 2am, his audience still waiting. There was no electricity but the moon shone down like a spotlight on Menano who, wrapped in his student gown, appeared almost ethereal.[11]

He gave his last concert in Coimbra on 25 June 1967, received the prestigious 'Ordem de Santiago' decoration from the Portuguese government the following year and died, aged 74, on 11 November 1969.

Perhaps more than anyone, including de Bettencourt, Menano represents the essence of Coimbra Fado. His dual role as conservative traditionalist and breathtaking innovator is a complex one that can still generate resentment among aficionados. That he sang within a traditional framework is undeniable – 'Fado de Sa Velha', 'Fado do Choupal' and 'Fado Hilario' bear eloquent testimony to his tradionalist approach. However, he was also insightful enough to realise that the context and form of the Fado could be expanded to include subjects that lay outside of Coimbra. 'Fado Alentejano' and 'Fado da Beira' sing of the beauty of Portuguese countryside a long way from the cloistered university atmosphere. He further realised that the Fado could travel and be appreciated by other cultures. His trips to France, Spain and Germany were as much about taking Portuguese culture into new areas as they were about celebrating it in the Lusophone world. Today his reputation remains undiminished; three compact discs, representing the bulk of his work, newly remastered and handsomely illustrated with original sheet music, sit in Valentim de Carvalho's catalogue and were, upon their launch, advertised on Portuguese television.

Of other contemporaries, Alexandre de Rezende, Francisco Caetano and Mário de Fonseca all contributed to both the flowering of the Coimbra Fado and also in no small measure to defining it for future generations. Rezende, who recorded in 1927 for Odeon's Parlophon record label, was a prolific writer who added a number of songs to the general catalogue of Coimbra Fado, while Caetano, accompanied by his brothers Alberto and José, produced a collection of twelve songs for Columbia that are among the most archaic performances on record, and may actually reflect aspects of a lost style from the nineteenth century.

Fonseca is mentioned by American travel writer Lawton McCaul in a fascinating, if perhaps slightly romanticized, passage from his 1931 book *Portugal For Two*:

> Dr. de Serra has squandered time upon us, taken us places, and been to no end of trouble on our behalf. The other day, I asked him if he would be so kind as to tell me the titles of some good Fados, as we'd like to get gramophone records of them. Immediately he offered to accompany us to the shop. So we had only to sit and listen while, at his command, the latest and most fascinating numbers were played for us.
>
> 'Aha, this is the best!' he commented when a Fado of Coimbra was put on. 'It is by Dr. Fonseca, one of my BIG friends. A doctor of music?' 'No, a doctor of law. We in our profession like to think that we have the best singers and guitar players, and I believe you will find it is true. This next one is by another big friend, a judge of the Municipal Court. A good singer, isn't he?'
>
> No denying it, his honour rendered beyond exception. By the time we had picked our bouquet of troubadourings we were indebted to Dr. de Serra for an acquaintance with the Portuguese Bar. Even the guitar duets we chose, as much by our personal preference as by guidance, were found to be strictly legal.[12]

The Coimbra Guitarra Tradition

The 'guitar duets' that McCaul mentioned are the other side of the Coimbra Fado coin; inextricably woven into the vocal tradition, they have nevertheless developed and maintained a character of their own. In essence they are not duets, but virtuoso performances upon the guitarra, underpinned by a simple yet essential viola accompaniment. Their development runs parallel with that of the vocal style and should be seen as a part of the Coimbra Fado tradition. Just as their counterparts did in Lisbon, Coimbra guitarristas produced an endless stream of variacose (variations) in both major and minor keys. These solos, while of necessity bearing the same titles (*Variações em do menor, em fa maior, em la menor* etc.), differ widely from each other and become an artist's personal statement.

The origins of the guitarra tradition are to be found, like the vocal tradition, in the introduction of the Fado from Lisbon during the latter half of the nineteenth century. Who the first virtuoso guitarra player was remains unclear. Possibly it was Anthero da Veiga, born in 1866, a student at Coimbra by 1885 and therefore a contemporary of Hilario. António Brojo provided the following description of da Veiga:

> A prominent guitarra virtuoso and pioneer of the instrumental tradition in Coimbra. An avid collector of Portuguese rural musical traditions, he incorporated some of the melodies he collected within his instrumental compositions. 'Bailados do Minho', using melodies that accompanied dances from the northwest region traditionally designated Minho, is one of his best-known compositions.[13]

This interest in collecting and assimilating traditional folk tunes, apparently pioneered by da Veiga, permeated throughout Coimbra University. Da Veiga recorded just once, for Grand Bazaar/HMV, in 1927. By that time he was living in Spain, and was met there by H.E. Davidson, HMV's resident engineer on the Iberian peninsula. Da Veiga, accompanied by his son Eugenio, recorded 'Bailes Regionais Portugueses'(Regional Portuguese Dances), 'Canções Regionais Portugueses' (Regional Portuguese Songs), 'Fado Melodico' and 'Variaçoes Em Re Menor'. Prompted by letters of complaint from da Veiga in March 1929, Grand Bazaar finally issued all four sides on two sequentially coupled 78rpm discs in the late spring of 1930. They display a style that is fluid, assured and finely honed.

The themes contained within 'Cantos Regionais' and 'Bailes Regionais' reflect da Veiga's interest in collecting folk music, and probably point to his having influenced the direction that Coimbra virtuosi guitarra took in reinterpreting rustic folk themes. Certainly the tunes he preserved appear time and again in the collective Coimbra repertoire. Da Veiga was 61 when he was recorded, but he lived to be 94 years old and his influence is still acknowledged in Coimbra today.

Júlio Silva, da Veiga's contemporary, remains a shadowy figure who again recorded just once, in 1927. From the evidence of the one surviving photograph of him, he was a man in at least his sixties when he played eight tunes on the stage of the Teatro São Luís in Lisbon for the Gramophone Company. His choice of material was in some ways strikingly similar in character to da Veiga's; the ancient 'Fado Choradinho', 'Chula', 'Bailarico Saloio' and 'Ramaldeira' – all interpretive fantasias based upon traditional dances – two waltzes, a minuet and his own composition, 'Fado Melancólico' were played with flair and *élan*, coupled with an ease that belied their complexity.

If da Veiga and Silva were the 'fathers' of Coimbra guitarra, Artur Paredes was the favourite son. He came from a family of guitarristas and inherited his style from his father Gonçalvo and his uncle Manuel, both contemporaries of da Veiga and Silva. Again, Paredes recorded for Grand Bazaar/HMV, and was part of the group, including Paradella de Oliveira and Armando Goes, that came down to Lisbon in May 1927. Accompanied by Afonso de Sousa on second guitarra and Guillerme Barbosa on viola, Paredes performed eight tunes, including an instrumental version of 'Fado Hilario', da Veiga's 'Bailados do Minho', three variaçoes and his own 'Fantasia', a splendid reading of rural folk themes that further demonstrated da Veiga's influence.

Paredes, who had toured Brazil in 1925 with Menano, de Bettencourt, Junot and de Oliveira, spent much of his time composing, giving concerts in and around Coimbra and, from 1930 until 1933, involving himself in extraordinarily complex litigation with Grand Bazaar/HMV over the question of royalty payments on records issued in America. On 21 January 1930, Grand Bazaar's Mr Allen wrote to the Gramophone Company in Hayes:

> Mr. Paredes does not want to receive his royalties regarding records issued in America because he says he must receive the same royalty as that one your goodselves give him,

that is 10% on 25 escudos (our catalogue price), and not 5% on US $0.75, the Victor catalogue price.

His claim lies in the fact of your goodselves, by a special concession, having attributed his royalties regarding prices of the Portuguese catalogue and not regarding prices of your catalogue, as his contract clearly mentions; by this reason he wants to receive royalties on records sold in America referring to prices mentioned in our catalogues, and not Victor catalogues.

He also says that by some preliminary conversations we had with him, before the making out of his contract, he understood that same amount would be paid to him for each record sold out here in Portugal or in Portuguese America.

Although preliminary conversations do not affect the meaning of the contract, as our lawyer has explained to us, we can no doubt assure you that we did not make any affirmation of that kind.

The only thing we told Mr. Paredes was that, as the sales in America, principally in Brazil, ought to be much bigger than those here, the total amount he would receive for royalties on records issued by the Victor Company would more or less equal those he would receive for records sold in our territory.

Mr. Paredes has handed the solution of this question to his lawyers and we on our side have done the same.

Our lawyer says there is no doubt that Mr. Paredes has not got the slightest reason to put this question, and the fact is that, after our second letter our lawyers wrote to that one of Mr. Paredes, showing him the clauses mentioned in the contract signed by Cia. del Gramofono and that gentleman, he has given no answer.

In due course we will inform you of everything concerning the matter.[14]

The litigation went on for a further three years, and was finally settled in the municipal court of Coimbra, who awarded Paredes 1 643 escudos (£13/6/8d) on 25 September 1933. In an internal memo between Gramco's Hayes and Barcelona offices, Barcelona confirmed the settlement, adding 'We are glad to state that this affair has now found a satisfactory solution. Mr. Paredes has in fact accepted the royalties actually due to him, and the receipt signed by him no doubt should fully cover us against any future complications.'[15]

Clearly a case of principle rather than money, as far as Paredes was concerned. If, indeed, he did settle for 5% royalties on his American sales, as the memo suggests, it represents 1413 copies of his records sold in Victor's territory, principally North America and Brazil.

Paredes' son Carlos carried his father's tradition into the next generation and, despite falling foul of Salazar's government and spending some years as a political prisoner, he became the figurehead of Coimbra guitarra playing from the 1960s until his health forced a gradual retirement through the 1980s. The recordings he and his father made collaboratively during the 1970s find both men still in possession of their creative powers. Artur Paredes died at Coimbra in 1980.

*   *   *

The Fado Tradition in Porto

Though not the capital, Porto has the distinction of having bestowed on the whole country its ancient name of Portus Cale. Like Lisbon, it is impressive less on account of individual monuments than of its general situation and appearance. Crossing by one of the two lofty bridges over the Douro river to the British wine lodges at Vila Nova de Gaia, the traveller is rewarded with a view which has altered little since Wellington in 1809 forced the passage of the river in the teeth of the French.

On the opposite side of the gorge rises the city with countless miniature gardens inlaid among its red roofs and grey walls. It culminates in two steep hills, crowned the one by a Romanesque cathedral and the other by the tall Clerigos tower. The spacious squares and avenues of modern development are hidden behind this spectacular drop curtain, and the old Oporto of the river bank is as unspoilt at close quarters as from a distance. The predominance of granite lends the city a more sober appearance than Lisbon, but the street life is no less exuberant.[16]

It has been impossible to establish a case for the existence of anything resembling a proletarian 'Porto Style' within the framework of the Fado. Between 1904 and 1920 recordings were made there by Beka, Odeon and Gramophone Company Ltd, but the music they captured was a mixture of the theatre and cafe styles prevalent in Lisbon at that time. José Bacalhau, an important early poet-Fadista, recorded there and Madalena de Mello, whose career in the Lisbon Fado Houses would last for over two decades, was born there and is described as singing 'with a Porto accent', [17] but none of this culminated in the achievement of a distinct Porto style.

However, the University at Porto did possess something of a Fado tradition. It has been almost completely overlooked, and its practitioners often mistaken for Coimbra artists, so similar is its approach and sentiment. Due, thankfully, to the activities of competitive record companies the Porto tradition, like that of Coimbra, was captured on disc in the 1920s. At the request of their agent Ricardo Lemos, the Odeon-owned Parlophon label held one 1927 session in Lisbon to record the singer Carlos Leal, his supporting musicians Armando Marques, Pais Da Silva and Francisco Fernandes, the guitarrista Ernesto Brandão accompanied by José Taveira on viola, and the group led by guitarrista António Coelho supported by the guitarrista António Martins and the viola player Augusto Nogueira that Parlophon called simply 'Trio de Guitarras e Viola'. The style, in all cases, is indistinguishable from that of Coimbra. There is some evidence, in the Porto-based students' magazine 'O Tripeiro', of a measure of co-operation and interest between the Porto and Coimbra schools. It reported, on 6 May 1928, that a gala show had been held at the São João Theatre, the largest in Porto, featuring Coimbra singers Paradella de Oliveira and Armando Goes alongside Carlos Leal and Ferreira da Silva from Porto.

Carlos Alberto Leal was born around the turn of the century in Vila do Conde, five miles north of Porto, and grew up under the tutelage of his father, a musician with a reportedly beautiful voice. At Porto University he became part of a group who practised the Fado on a regular basis. In 1962, Dr Amando Marques, a key figure in the original group, wrote an article in the *Porto Académico* newspaper that vividly, if somewhat rosily, recalled the experience of the Porto University Fadistas:

It's been some decades since, and time flows unnoticed! All of us were 'Cape and Gown' (i.e. students) and the good folk of the town enjoyed seeing it and cherished it. Life ran quietly, simple, loyal, always full of honesty in our common relations. We had the Academical Association (a students social club), we had gone through the Great War of 1914–18, and that event had shaken us deeply but got us nearer to a better understanding of one another. The student tried to keep and strengthen a tradition, by his own academical life and most of all by promoting his festivities to which the Porto people were associated, thus creating a student's tradition.

I will mention just a few names as representatives of them all. There were poets like Carlos Cochofel and Figueira Lopes; playwrites Adalberto Mendo, Augusto Farinhas, Perry Garcia and Zeferino Moura. Actors and humourists João Ribeiro, António Mendes and Joaquim Bravo.

There was no lack of guitarristas and excellent singers of Fados, like Aires Pinto Ribeiro, a brilliant guitarist, Ernesto Brandão, Cicero de Azevedo, Manuel Pereira Leite. Great singers like José Taveira, Mario Delgado Viemonte, Cabral Borges, and Carlos Leal!

It was a time of glory for the university. Art and humour were joined together and friendships were even more deep. José Taveira and Carlos Leal were brilliant soloists for their own merits, for their strong, melodious charming and melancholic voices.

The group enlarged, being more united, with Francisco Fernandes, José Fernandes, another writer, Alberto de Serpa, Alberto do Carmo Machado, who was a cadet sergeant and António Abrantes. We rehearsed the guitarradas and Fados. Carlos Leal sang the beautiful Fados and songs with his melodious, clear, sharp voice:

My eyes depart
So sad for you, my dear!
That you never saw eyes
So sad for anyone

Serenades were made anywhere in town as well as outside in Braga, Vila do Conde, Povoa do Varzim and so on. We very seldom knew the lady we were singing and playing for!

No authority would intercept us. The serenades were made at 2 or 3 am when the town was sound asleep! Everyone enjoyed it, when they heard Carlos Leal's voice and the group wrapped in capes and gowns that silently released the meloncholical chords from their guitarras. Leal's voice rose softly in the air and echoed against the sides of the street, without breaking the atmosphere's silence or interrupting the dreams of whoever was dreaming.

It was a dreamlike awakening. Windows opened, nightgowns were seen amidst the dim light and silence which surrounded us. Leal always sang serenades, as José Taveira and Cabral Borges often did. It was me who would go to the police comissioner, the late Dr. Lopes Carneiro, to ask for the due permit. Always in cape and gown (I never wore anything else) he already knew, when I entered his office:

'What, do you want Marques? I know, it's a serenade; where is it?'
(he picks up the phone to make a call)

'Please tell this area that the students with Marques and Leal are going to make a serenade; They should not be disturbed!'

Soon we would have a large audience which would not go away! Our names were known all over town, especially by the girls. When the serenade was over each one would go home after a wonderful night, well spent, without any conflict whatsoever and everyone enjoyed this romantic night show. The voice and feeling Carlos Leal put into his Fados were each time, year after year, better and more expressive, him singing with more soul. In Porto, Coimbra, all over Portugal, in Spain, Carlos Leal was the Academy's hero of that time. Following an idea of the students who had, like me, come from Porto to the University of Coimbra, Porto's Academy were invited to go to Coimbra. It was glory! They spent nothing, they were lodged at the Republica (traditional community houses for students) and at several houses. The recitals were an artistic success. Carlos Leal and other academic artists had their triumph there, in Coimbra.

Accompanied on the guitarra by me and by Francisco Fernandes – today a distinguished surgeon in Mozambique – and on the viola by Pais da Silva, Carlos Leal made several records that were soon sold out, like the famous 'Canção das Rendilheiras'. He always co-operated at the revues, at the parades, at the shows the Academy would organise. He was esteemed and modest, always meeting requests for his serenades, Carlos Leal graduated from medical school and came to practical life, the profession, the struggle. The esteem and brotherly friendship that joined us kept the same until his death.

His life ceased at April 9th 1960, in the prime of life! This fine lad, loyal in name ['Leal' means 'Loyal' in Portuguese] and in acts with honest ways, a very distinguished professional, became a sick man, miserable, having suffered the loss of his charming wife eight months earlier, whom he loved so much, dies passionately as a romantic, an emotional man for disposition and psychological structure leaving us with an emptiness and deep saudade.[18]

Leal himself, quoted in a 1938 article, corroborates Marques's colourful description of events, but adds a dark footnote that echoes the view of traditionalists in Lisbon:

What great saudade I feel when I remember the serenades at the dead of night by the streets of the town with Armando Marques, Pereira Leite and others. Besides the sentimental points, so many burlesque scenes full of natural and spontaneous comicality. Returning from these serenades and after terrible bullfighting with stray cats, we would end the night at the Transmontano, in Fadological sessions, under the guidance of old Mouzão, with his hair already white, and other devoted lovers of Fado and guitarra.

Then Fado died. Died because of the gramophone and radio. It was this gramophonotherapy and radiotherapy that, being given in such high doses, provoked dyspepsia and nausea in everybody.[19]

Outside of this group, only José Joaquim Cavalheiro, a guitarrista of astonishing virtuosity, and his partner on viola, J. Campos, are known to have been Porto University musicians. Cavalheiro's recordings, for HMV in 1927 and Polydor two years later, rival the best that Coimbra has ever produced, but the evidence to prove that he was either part of a larger group or a lone phenomenon simply does not exist.

While the Porto tradition completely fell from public attention after its brief flirtation with recorded fame, the Coimbra Fado tradition continued. Unrecorded from 1931, with Menano's last appearance in a recording studio, until the early 1950s, it remained a cloistered and protected music, as its sporadic appearance on record until the present time proves. In 1952 António Brojo founded the Quartetto de Guitarras de Coimbra with António Portugal, Dr Aurelio Reis and Mario de Castro. Their aim was to keep alive the traditions of Coimbra instrumentalists, and especially to perform the collected works of Anthero da Veiga.

They recorded one 78rpm coupling for Melodia records, and, at the same 1953 session, accompanied singers Fernando Rolim and José Afonso. With some changes, Brojo kept the quartet together, still retaining António Portugal, until at least 1980. They surfaced once more on disc, recording for the American Folkways company in the late 1960s.

A Coimbra Fado today – one can hear it sung at the Café Santa Cruz or the Bar Diligencia – remains faithful to the original vision of Menano and de Bettencourt's interpretations. Lisbon aficionados will argue that the Coimbra style is not Fado at all, but within the confines of this ancient university city, you will find that view derided and, moreover, you will experience a music that has remained pure and unadulterated for nearly a century.

Notes

1. Rodney Gallop (1936), *Portugal – A Book of Folkways*, Cambridge: CUP.
2. Ibid.
3. Ibid.
4. Rodney Gallop (1931), 'Some Records of the Portuguese Fado', *The Gramophone*, October.
5. Rodney Gallop (1936), *Portugal – A Book of Folkways*, Cambridge: CUP.
6. Rodney Gallop (1931), 'Some Records of the Portuguese Fado', *The Gramophone*, October.
7. Zeca Afonso, quoted in a letter to the author by Caramaes.
8. Mario Martins, quoted in a letter to the author by Caramaes.
9. João Gaspar Simoes, quoted in a letter to the author by Caramaes.
10. From the Interstate collection.
11. João Gaspar Simoes, quoted in a letter to the author by Caramaes.
12. Lawton McCaul (1931), *Portugal for Two*, NYC: Dodd, Mead & Co.
13. Notes to Smithsonian-Fokways 'Musical Traditions of Portugal', SFWC40435.
14. GBDP to Hayes re Paredes, 1931/EMI Archives.
15. Hayes inter-office memo, 25.9.33/EMI Archives.
16. Rodney Gallop (1936), *Portugal – A Book of Folkways*, Cambridge: CUP.
17. João de Caramalho, quoted in a letter to the author by Caramaes.
18. Extract from the *Porto Acadêmico* journal, 1962.
19. Extract from the *Porto Acadêmico* journal, 1938.

5 The Media Industry

The first patent application for an audio recording and playback system was lodged in Washington D.C. in 1887 by Emile Berliner, and by about 1890 the first commercially produced recordings, offered as 5" diameter plates, were available to the public. The Gramophone Company of London (Gramco) and the Victor Company of Camden, New Jersey, commenced trading in 1897 and 1898 respectively and by 1900 the novelty was beginning to seize public imagination on an international scale. In the autumn of that year one of Gramco's technical engineers, the American, W. Sinkler Darby, recorded 67 performances on flat, 7" single-sided discs in Porto. None appear to have survived, and no catalogue has ever been found to provide clues as to the content of this premier recording expedition into Portugal. However, by 1904, Lisbon was a surprisingly active recording centre, with not only Gramco and its then arch-rival Odeon competing for the new market, but also a number of small, independent companies mushrooming in their wake.

The Odeon Company, founded in Berlin in November 1903 by Max Strauss and Heinrich Zuntz, quickly adopted an aggressive world-wide marketing stance in order to secure its survival. Regarded by Victor and Gramco as an upstart new-comer, Odeon was excluded from the deal that the two former companies had struck to share the world markets between them. This agreement gave Victor all of the Americas including Canada, the Caribbean, Japan, and most of the rest of Asia, while Gramco would have Europe, the Russian and Ottoman Empires, Africa, India, the Middle East and Australasia. China and parts of the Far East would be shared. They agreed not to interfere with each other's territory, and further, to exchange specific recordings for issue in their own areas. In this way, it was felt, Gramco could market the best American recordings and Victor would have access to both prestigious European operatic and classical material as well as 'ethnic' recordings in European languages to sell to the newly-arrived immigrants. At this stage, the record companies were also the makers of gramophones; the marketing of the two were inextricably linked and it was considered just as important to sell the machine as the record.

Odeon decided to blaze its own international trail, posing a significant threat to the other two companies. Like Gramco and Victor, Odeon manufactured both machines and records, but they seized the initiative in 1904 with the introduction of the double-sided disc. Previously all gramophone records, flat or cylindrical, had been single-sided. By offering a double-sided record for the same price, Odeon effectively halved the cost of buying records. Alarm quickly spread throughout the industry:

> I must draw your attention to the fact that these new Odeon records are doing us a lot of harm. Our travellers meet them everywhere and our agents do not stick to their contracts to sell only Gramco and Zono. They say the public insists on having those double-sided records because they are only half the price of ours, and much larger in proportion. If we do not want to lose our trade then something must be done to cut the Odeon out.[1]

Odeon founded its empire using the sound strategy that a local entrepreneur will better understand his own market than a representative transplanted from head office. In Portugal they found Ricardo Lemos, whose retail shop at Rua Formosa 304 in Porto dealt in bicycles, batteries and mechanical devices – including gramophones. Lemos had already approached Gramco with the suggestion of becoming their exclusive agent, only to be told that this would be impossible as the Paris office of Gramco was already handling the territory. Lemos therefore set about his newly-appointed task for Odeon with a zeal that unnerved the competition. Within a very short space of time he had found and contracted a number of smaller retail outlets throughout Portugal to take Odeon products exclusively. He also arranged recording sessions both in Porto and Lisbon, the Berlin-based head office giving him almost total artistic control and backing him up by supplying a recording engineer and equipment.

Between 1904 and 1915 Odeon and Lemos found themselves competing not only with British Gramco but also with the French 'Simplex' and 'Ideal' companies, the German-owned 'Favourit' and 'Beka' labels, and the locally-owned 'Luzofone' and 'Chiadofone'. Of these, the Germans were most active. Beka, who made a massive recording expedition to Lisbon and Porto in 1904, started marketing their product the following year. Favourit and Ideal joined the market in 1910, Simplex a year later. By 1915 the Portuguese public was faced with a wide choice of recordings, mostly of theatrical performances with orchestral accompaniment, but also a few cafe singers accompanied by guitarra.

Of those few, Reynaldo Varella was by far the most prolific. A singer, songwriter and guitarrista, he recorded at least 140 songs for nine different record companies, including all the major internationals, between 1903 and 1915. He is important because his repertoire includes the first recorded versions of seminal songs like 'Fado Robles' and 'Fado do Ganga'. His style was essentially that of the Lisbon Cafe, but his eclecticism allowed him to include topics beyond the boundaries of the city, and he sang of Coimbra, Estoril, Funchal and Alentejo. There is some evidence to suggest that he was a native of Madeira – sheet music of the period refers to his having composed several songs on the island – but no proven biographical details have survived.

The years 1904 to 1925 represented a particularly free and open period for the Portuguese record industry. Artists were paid a few escudos per recorded side and royalty contracts were simply never offered. As a result, performers like Varella would often appear simultaneously on a number of labels, singing the same material. There was also some evidence of pirating; Chiadofone records were actually pressings by other companies with a Chiadofone logo crudely glued to the top half of the label, obscuring the original trade marks. Operated from a retail shop in Lisbon's Chiado district, they were aimed at theatre-goers and appear to have had little distribution outside of Lisbon. The French Simplex company incorporated an anti-pirating device at the start of each of their records. A male voice would shout 'DISQUES SIMPLEX' just before the music began, establishing beyond question whose recording it really was.

Luzofone, operating between 1910 and 1916, just a few streets away from Chiadofone, were at least a legitimate organization, although they appear to have done little, if any, of their own recording. Their records were pressed for them by Simplex in Paris, using Simplex masters, but sporting their own handsome tricolour logo on a properly produced label. Their repertoire consisted, as did everybody else's, of theatrical hits from the revistas of the day mixed with a smattering of cafe artists. Luzofone's business folded in 1916, probably as a result of the deepening crisis on the western front and the difficulty of arranging pressings in a country that was embroiled in war.

For the first quarter of the twentieth century, Fados in sheet music format sold in much larger quantities than records. Surviving examples from the period 1900 to 1920 appear to indicate a number of small, semi-private publishers operating on a local level. It is certain that in 1920 Valentim de Carvalho, one of Lisbon's oldest and most revered music shops, published some Fados, and may have done so earlier, but from either 1921 or 1922, Sassetti & Ca., located at 56 Rua do Carmo, just a few streets from Carvalho, commenced an operation that would, in the following decades, publish over 95% of all sheet music sold both in Portugal and, through affiliates, in Brazil. They employed a British commercial artist called Stuart, resident in Lisbon, to illustrate the covers of their editions. He produced, for at least the two decades between 1922 and 1942, an arresting series of graphics, often employing muted reds and greens, or starkly contrasting red and black, that both captured and defined the mood of the period and have helped to fix the visual image of early Fado in the public mind. Sassetti were almost certainly in some form of partnership with Valentim de Carvalho, since Carvalho's own publishing activities ceased at about the same time Sassetti's commenced, and all published Carvalho recordings were handled by Sassetti.

Until the mid-1920s, recorded Fados were aimed at audiences of middle-income and above, the cost of a gramophone putting it out of reach of the bulk of the workforce. This meant that the style heard on record before 1925 was either that of revista artists like Júlia Mendes, Maria Victoria and Delphina Victor, or of the mostly male intellectual amateurs, whose approach was often somewhat stiff and distant. Although there was plenty of raw emotion in the street and cafe performances of the time, only a little was available on record. Reynaldo Varella, for all his eclecticism, was closer to the middle-class salon than the proletariat tavern.

*   *   *

In 1925 a revolution in technology set in motion events that would change the face of recorded music. The American Western Electric company, following some years of research, announced the successful development of the moving coil microphone recording system. This allowed the entire recording process to be carried out electrically rather than acoustically, with huge advances not only in audio quality but also durability and cost effectiveness. The new electric masters would not wear out as quickly as acoustic ones did. The sound was louder and carried greater fidelity. More importantly, the records could now be pressed in much larger quantities than before, and therefore sold cheaply, creating mass-market opportunities that had previously been impossible.

The new records could be played on existing equipment, but with the parallel development of cheap, portable machines on which to play them, recorded music suddenly ceased to be an exclusive amusement for the rich. Western Electric originally offered to lease the system to American Columbia, but, near bankruptcy at the time, Columbia were unable to raise the funds. Sensing impending disaster unless he moved quickly, Louis Sterling, the American-born head of the English branch of Columbia, raised capital from London banks, immediately bought out his parent company and leased the new system. The following year he purchased the Odeon company, forming an empire that threatened Gramco more directly than Odeon itself had ever done.

Flushed with success, redoubling efforts for world domination, and needing an agent to handle its affairs in Portugal, Columbia started looking for someone reliable. They found Valentim de Carvalho on Rua Nova da Almada in Lisbon. This had been a family business since 1824, establishing itself as the premier retail outlet for pianos, wind, brass and string instruments and sheet music. It now also sold gramophones, accessories and records.

The deal that Columbia offered Carvalho was modelled upon the Odeon plan, giving Carvalho the artistic control to find, sign and rehearse the artists. The terms of the contract between Columbia and Carvalho say much about the way in which record industry business was conducted at this time. It is interesting to note, in the following extracts from the original contract, written by Columbia lawyers, how heavily weighted in favour of Columbia the document was.

TERRITORY OF REPRESENTATION

1.   COLUMBIA grants to CARVALHO the sole agency for Portugal, Madeira, Azores and Portuguese West Africa.
2.   COLUMBIA grants this agency to CARVALHO on the distinct understanding that CARVALHO does not enter into any other agency agreement for distribution of records, gramophones and radios during the period of this control other than agencies he already holds.
3.   CARVALHO is not entitled to effect sales in any territory either directly or indirectly, other than that for which he has obtained the agency of COLUMBIA. He

is liable to make good to COLUMBIA any loss which the latter may incur through the non-observance of this express stipulation.

OBJECT OF CONTRACT

1. The agency covers the gramophone records and talking machines and radio marketed by COLUMBIA under the trade-mark COLUMBIA, and also parts and accessories, so far as such are at the free disposal of COLUMBIA.
2. COLUMBIA undertakes to refer to CARVALHO all enquiries and orders which it receives relative to COLUMBIA in the territories assigned to CARVALHO.

MINIMUM TURNOVER

1. CARVALHO undertakes to purchase from Columbia during the currency of this contract the following minimum quantities, delivery to be effected in approximately equal monthly payments.

    1st Contract Year .... 20,000 Columbia records
    2nd   "   "   40,000   "   "
    3rd   "   "   50,000   "   "

RECORDING

1. CARVALHO agrees to have made for COLUMBIA in Portugal at least two recording expeditions per year, and to make not less than 30 titles per expedition.
2. COLUMBIA retains legal ownership of all recordings (including galvanic copies and pressing matrices). However COLUMBIA is not entitled to supply these recordings under any trade mark whatsoever to anyone other than CARVALHO in his territory during the currency of the contract. For new recordings, CARVALHO must give a minimum order of 200 per title.
3. CARVALHO admits that although the recording expenses in his territory have to be paid by him, such expenses are, *de facto*, met by COLUMBIA as the latter has taken this circumstance into consideration when fixing the prices to be paid by CARVALHO for his records.

PRICES

1. For all records in the standard series COLUMBIA will charge CARVALHO 1/1d (one shilling and one penny) for the 10-inch and 1/9d (one shilling and nine pence) for the 12-inch nett. For all other series COLUMBIA will give CARVALHO a discount of 50% and 10% (fifty per cent and ten per cent) from the English retail price ruling at the date of this contract. These records are F.O.B London. Copyright will be charged extra.
2. Any artists royalties in Portuguese records made under contracts or which have to be paid in future on records which may be recorded later by CARVALHO either under new contracts or under contracts now existing, and sold by CARVALHO in the territory named in this contract are to be paid by CARVALHO.
3. The prices for records are subject to alteration, particularly if there is any change in the duty as at present charged in Portugal or in the event that COLUMBIA can

supply a record to CARVALHO of a lighter weight which will make a reduction in his landed costs.

TERMS OF PAYMENT

1.   Terms of payment are cash against documents.

COPYRIGHT

1.   CARVALHO assumes full responsibility both personally and towards COLUMBIA for any prejudice which the latter may suffer through contravention of the copyright regulations in connection with the records recorded by him for COLUMBIA.
2.   CARVALHO must not make or cause to be made for COLUMBIA any recordings for which the copyright payable to the owners of the music or words shall exceed 3¼% of the full retail price of the double-sided record.
3.   CARVALHO agrees that all works purchased by him either now or at any future date shall be accessible for use by COLUMBIA, its sister companies, or any other company which COLUMBIA may designate during the entire term of the copyright against payment of the stipulated license, which shall not exceed 3¼% of the retail price of the double-sided record, even should it be that CARVALHO may cease to act as agent of the Columbia Company at any future date.

ADVERTISING

1.   COLUMBIA will make CARVALHO an allowance of 50% (fifty per cent) of all monies spent in newspaper advertising for the first year and 33% (thirty-three per cent) for the next two years. This allowance applies exclusively to newspaper advertising and the advertisements must refer solely and only to COLUMBIA goods. The credits will be passed to CARVALHO on receipt by COLUMBIA of the receipted invoices from the newspaper people with copies of the newspaper attached.
2.   COLUMBIA will supply CARVALHO with electros of all sizes for newspaper advertising, and will furthermore supply him with samples of all posters and streamers etc, so that CARVALHO can call for quantities in accordance with his requirements. Such quantities will be supplied free of charge.
3.   CARVALHO agrees to bring out regularly every two months a supplement containing only COLUMBIA records, printed in Portuguese, of all COLUMBIA records which he will offer for sale.

RETURN OF RECORDS

1.   CARVALHO may return up to 10% (ten per cent) of his purchases together with an order for a similar quantity of equal record size and category. No credit will be passed for returned records, but new records will be supplied at a nett price of 8d. (eight pence) for 10-inch and 1/- (one shilling) for 12-inch.
2.   All expenses occasioned by the return of records are for the account of CARVALHO, and it is definitely understood that such returns only apply to perfect and saleable records, and not to records which have been broken or damaged in any way. Records may be returned half-yearly or quarterly but the returns may not

exceed 10% (ten per cent) yearly of the purchases during any contract year. If the 10% is not taken up in any year, the balance cannot be carried forward.

DURATION OF CONTRACT

1. This contract comes into operation at its signature and runs for a period of three years.

SELLING PRICES

1. CARVALHO agrees to fix, in agreement with COLUMBIA, the retail prices at which COLUMBIA products will be sold in the agency territory, and to see that these prices are rigidly maintained by all his dealers and agents.
2. CARVALHO also guarantees that in the event of his contract being broken at any time for any reason, he will not dispose of his COLUMBIA stocks below the retail price.

With this somewhat loaded contract duly signed, the initial recording sessions took place in August 1926 in an upper room at Carvalho's head office on Rua Nova da Almada. They were the first electric recordings ever made in Portugal and an impressive array of talent had been assembled by Carvalho's staff. The immensely popular Adelina Fernandes recorded 25 titles that month. Salgado Armando Freire, who would later record under his more famous sobriquet Armandinho, cut six instrumentals with his partner Georgino de Sousa. Alberto Costa, accompanied by Freire and de Sousa, sang twelve songs and Estevão Amarante, the well-loved theatre artist, produced several genuine Fados, his first recordings since 1915. Other lesser-known Lisbon artists also made records that would be released on the J- prefix series that Columbia had reserved for its Portuguese artists.

This wave of activity left Gramco somewhat marginalized even though it too had leased the Western Electric system. The fact that it continued to run its Portuguese operation from the Paris office on Boulevard Richard-Lenoir didn't improve matters. The mood was one of intransigence:

> I have found that as a result of the visit paid by Mr. D'Arcey-Evans to Lisbon during November of 1923, a decision was reached here to the effect that it would not be possible to appoint an agent to that country, and that the only way in which business could be carried on there, was for the Gramophone Cy at Hayes or Compagnie Française du Gramophone in Paris, to execute all orders which reach them from Portuguese customers, provided that such orders were accompanied by cash.[2]

In January 1926 a Portuguese entrepreneur called Nunes dos Santos resubmitted a proposal to Paris offering, for the second time, to become recording and distribution agent for the company. In February, Paris forwarded the proposal to the companies head office in Hayes, Middlesex, along with their own thoughts on the subject:

We feel obliged to forward for your consideration an outline of some of the conditions obtaining with reference to the expansion of the Trade-Mark in PORTUGAL in so far as it may be affected by a French or Spanish source of supply, tending to indicate the advantage of the former, as layed before us by the Paris agent of the firm of Nunes dos Santos. The outline may of course be prompted in some measure by self-interest, but this we must leave to your appreciation.

1. NATIONAL FEELING. – In determining the likelihood of success as between a Portuguese agency run from Paris and one run from Barcelona, it would be wise not to neglect the moral factor, viz. the anti-Spanish feeling general among the Portuguese people who do all in their power to boycott Spanish goods. Prior to 1640, Portugal was under the heel of Spain. Now the Portuguese seek to demonstrate that they can get along very well without goods of Spanish origin. There is no trace of anti-French feeling in Portugal.
2. TRANSPORT. – Transport from Barcelona to any part of Portugal is proverbially slow and even an urgent order may take five or six weeks to be delivered, as several shipments are necessary. Goods from Paris are delivered in Lisbon 48 hours after reception at the address of the Paris agency. This prompt delivery is an invaluable aid to business.
3. CUSTOMS. – The normal procedure is for goods coming from Spain to be examined at Villa-Formosa at the Portuguese boundary. The risk of theft and breakage of records on repacking is considerable, to say nothing of the delay. French goods are sent in sealed waggons from Paris under care of the Wagons-Lits Company, and the customs formalities take place on arrival at Lisbon, where, as a matter of fact, the packages for Nunes dos Santos are rarely opened.
4. EXCHANGE. – The high peseta rate has a discouraging effect on trade between Portugal and Spain.

Should the outline prove to be well-founded, it would appear that GRAMOPHONE interests in the broad sense would be better served by supplying Portugal from FRANCE.

Yours Faithfully Cie Française du Gramophone[3]

Sensing that things were slipping beyond their control, and heeding the hard-earned lessons it had learned from Columbia and Odeon, Hayes responded by sending an executive called S.H. Sheard to investigate the situation in March. The result was that the dos Santos proposal was rejected in favour of one offered to Sheard by A.A. Allen, a chief executive of Grand Bazaar do Porto Lda. (GBDP).

GBDP's headed notepaper announced that it dealt in 'Gramophone records, toys, perfumes and novelties'. It also sold electrical and other household goods and undertook repairs to gramophones. With its main store and head office at Rua St. Catarina in Porto, a branch in Lisbon at Rua Augusta, a booming wine industry on its doorstep and facilities to ship goods in from England directly to Porto by steamer, it was felt that GBDP was the ideal company to represent Gramco's Portuguese interests. The English understood that the Portuguese did not trust the Spanish but they took the view that there had always been cordial relations between Britain and Portugal and that there was no need to delegate responsibility for a growth market in a pro-British country to the French.

Sheard and Allen reached an agreement that broadly reflected the terms between Columbia and Valentim de Carvalho. GBDP would undertake the duties of main agent for all Gramco goods – machines, accessories, spares and records – in the Portuguese territories, using their own retail outlets and supplying goods at agreed wholesale prices to independent shops in areas outside of Porto and Lisbon. Allen made it clear that a fresh batch of recordings were absolutely necessary to launch the new business and Sheard agreed. GBDP would be responsible for all artistic decisions, and Gramco would supply the expertise to turn out the finished product.

On 13 May 1927 H.E. Davidson, Gramco's resident recording engineer in Spain, arrived in Lisbon. He stayed a week and collected 30 titles by eight artists, five of whom – Armando Goes, Artur Paredes, Júlio Silva, Paradella de Oliveira and José Dias – were from Coimbra. It was the start of an ambitious programme involving artists from both Lisbon and Coimbra, that would extend over the next three years. Legally binding contracts with stated fees and royalty payments were offered to all the artists. A standard contract ran for a minimum period of one year, with an option controlled by the company, and specifically excluded the artists from recording for any other company during that time. It also allowed the company to lease material to American Victor, and guaranteed a reasonable fee or royalty to the artist.

When the 1927 recordings were issued on the plum-coloured EQ series label that Gramco allocated to its Portuguese issues, the record industry was entering a world-wide boom period that would last for almost three years. All the economic indicators pointed toward a steady growth of trade. The international stock market was buoyant and with little real threat of global conflict there was every reason to be confident. The first batch of records was well received by the public; in Porto the wine trade remained stable and a significant number of *nouveaux riches* merchants rewarded themselves by taking up the increasingly popular hobby of gramophone entertainment. For GBDP it was a good start to a short golden period. They could not have known then how bitter the ending would be.

*   *   *

From the beginning, GBDP faced a plethora of competition. Besides Columbia-Odeon, the German Brunswick-Polydor, Clausophon and Homokord companies all entered the market between 1925 and 1929. French Pathé had been in Portugal since the beginning but did little business; they sold less than 750 records nation-wide in the first half of 1928 and had dropped out by the end of that year. Homokord did twice that amount of business in the same period but in 1929, having lost their star artist, Adelina Fernandes, sold only 39 records by the end of the second quarter. They too withdrew from the market. Brunswick-Polydor, backed by its American parent company, launched two Portuguese series, one on each label, in 1929. They immediately recorded a number of popular Fadistas including Maria Alice, Cardoso Pessoa, Mariamélia and Lino Teixeira. Their combined sales figures for Portuguese artists in 1929 were 67,912 records, compared with HMV's 36,749, Odeon's 24,714 and Columbia's 15,309. It was quite clear who led the market for Fados. Fortunately for their competitors, Brunswick pulled out of the German and Portuguese markets in 1931 when the parent company changed hands in America.

The details of Clausophone's operations remain vague. They almost certainly recorded in Lisbon, then pressed their records in Germany and shipped back finished product to Portugal. They appear to have operated in Portugal for about three years, until the parent company went into liquidation in 1931. Clausophone recorded a broad cross section of Lisbon artists including well-established singers like Madalena de Mello, Maria Emelia Ferreira, Alfredo Ruas and António Vasconcellos.

However, GBDP had the backing of the HMV international catalogue to aid its sales. It was able to draw upon not only its specifically recorded Portuguese repertoire, but also the existing catalogues of popular English, French, Italian and Spanish recordings as well as selected masters leased by Gramco from American Victor. Thus, GBDP's 1928 general catalogue offered Portuguese Fados, folkloric recordings and current theatre hits and a wide range of American and English dance bands, Argentine tangos, Cuban sons, Brazilian sambas, French chansons and Italian opera.

The same was broadly true for Valentim de Carvalho, who could offer anything that the British parent company issued. Carvalho also made a concerted attempt, throughout 1927 and 1928, to capture the market for Coimbra Fado; they had the hugely popular Edmundo de Bettencourt and, furthermore, engaged in extensive recordings of instrumental guitarristas including many sides by Dr Ricardo Borges de Sousa, a vastly respected musician old enough to have been active at the beginning of the century. Nevertheless, the sales figures quoted above speak for themselves; Columbia product was trailing badly.

By the middle of 1929, however, some problems were also starting to emerge for GBDP:

> Due to the absence of some artists, only today are we able to send you our recording programme, which we hope will meet with your approval.
> The cost of the guitarra accompaniment is higher this year, due to the price now established by the competition, that we are obliged to follow.[4]

By early February 1930, with the shock waves of the Wall Street crash starting to take effect, things looked bleaker still. Disappointing sales had resulted in GBDP cancelling their contracts with Armando Goes and Paradella de Oliveira among others. Confronted with Hayes' reluctance, in uncertain economic circumstances, to make new recordings in Portugal, Allen wrote:

> I beg to call your attention to the present state of trade in our country which is very bad, affecting rather much our sales but also you very well understand that if we are to continue in the leadership of the gramophone in Portugal, we must accompany competition. I must inform you that competition is working hard as possible to get a leading position, publishing all hits that appear and allowing much bigger discounts than we are able.
> So how can we in future trading continue leading the trade if we have not regular issues of good Portuguese hits, granting at the same time smaller discounts to our

dealers? We quite well see that for you it is rather heavy to pay for recordings that bring you no profit but, as we have already informed you we are quite willing to undertake expenses of same.[5]

Despite their being less than 50 retail record outlets left operating in Portugal, Hayes agreed – given that their expenses would be lower – to hold another recording session in June. In the meantime, GBDP saw apparent saviours on the horizon; in a mood of almost evangelical glee Allen wrote in July 1930:

The interest for wireless is increasing rapidly in our territory. Some time ago we hardly had any broadcasting stations but now we have several in Oporto and Lisbon. Four of them principally, two in Lisbon and two in Oporto, have taken a leading position and are every day improving.

We have made arrangements with these broadcasting stations so that they will at least once a week broadcast our records. This is very interesting for us as they advertise our records and our products; after this policy was adopted we have noted an increase in our sales of those records that are broadcast.

When we issue a fresh lot of records we have them all broadcast with very successful results. The, perhaps best of these stations, C.T.1-B.O., in Lisboa, is regularly broadcasting our records and has programmes made out with their concerts.

Our Maestro (A&R man), Frederico de Freitas, organized in this broadcasting station, on 13th inst, absolutely free, a concert with some of our artists that recorded for us during the last recording period. This concert was a great success, and nearly every number had to be repeated as hundreds of persons telephoned to the station asking enthusiastically for several numbers to be sung again. Our Maestro's idea met with such good acceptance that he intends repeating these concerts every month, without, of course, bringing us any expense. [Participants in this broadcast included Madalena de Mello, Fernanda Coutinho and Corina Freire.]

In consequence, this concert brought hundreds of orders for records that were done out in the recent (June) session, We must say that the greater part of the success obtained with this concert was due to our Maestro's activity, organisation and the great interest he always takes in everything connected with your products. We profit the occasion to congratulate you and also ourselves for the splendid man you have as musical director in Portugal. Hoping you will appreciate the considerations contained herein.[6]

Such enthusiasm cut little ice at Gramco, however. On 29 September 1930, S.H. Sheard, clearly still GBDP's advocate, but equally clearly under internal pressure, wrote bluntly to Mr Allen:

For the year ending June 1930 our total sales to you of 10" and 12" plum and black label records amounted to 42, 892 and for the same period the recording expenses and artists' fees cost £2 647. This means that taking an average of 10" and 12" black and plum categories, every record supplied (whether Portuguese or otherwise) has cost the company in hard cash 14.811 pence for recording expenses alone.

To this alarming figure the following expenses have to be added; Artiste's royalties, copyright, cost of packing and advertising allowance.

After reading this confidential information you will not be surprised to learn that the company has made a very substantial loss on your record business.

This being the case I was strongly advised not to press the suggestions which I had formulated in regard to taking back records, extra advertising or any proposal involving the company in extra expenditure, but to recommend that you do your best with the new records when it is hoped a better result can be obtained.

At the same time I have been able to secure you one concession, namely an extension of your credit from 90 to 120 days. This has been granted as a temporary measure of relief owing to the present difficult times, and is to cover a period of twelve months.[7]

Allen replied on 4 October:

Your most kind letter of the 29th has come to hand and I most heartily thank you for the same.

I was absolutely certain that you would do your very best to try and help us overcome this crisis we are suffering, and in fact we now see that you have arranged for us the concession of the extension of our credits to 120 days, which is a great relief for us and a very important concession, for which I beg to express my very best thanks.

I am very sorry indeed to learn that your company is having a great loss with us, and so I understand very well the reason for you not having been able to secure the other concessions we had asked. You very well know, Mr. Sheard, that we have always done our very best for the sale of your goods, but we recently have been suffering from this tremendous and world round crisis and we have had to make with great sacrifice enormous reductions in our expenses to try and face the great slump in our sales.

I must confidentially inform you that our financial year, ended on 30th June last, showed us great losses on the Gramophone Branch.

The financial year we are now in, does not seem, up to the present, to be going any better, in spite of all the efforts we have done. It is necessary to know the actual trade conditions in Portugal to form a small idea of the difficulties we have to fight against. Our competitors are suffering perhaps harder still.

Let us hope that from now onwards, and with the arrival of the new very good Portuguese records, recently recorded, and that will soon be out on sale, things will begin getting better. This being so and with great favour of your company's assistance, which is due to your kind activity, we are confident we will overcome this serious situation.

In accordance with your telegram of yesterday, we telegraphed and are writing today to the Anglo South American Bank informing them that since the 1st October our credits will extend to 120 days from date. I am herewith enclosing a few snapshots of our car during his journey of 1800 km through the country visiting our dealers, etc, carrying 800 kilos of Gramophones, records and radio goods.

I am glad with the results obtained as we had good sales; imagine that in some places the car went the gramophone was unknown by the greater part of the population!

Before closing again I must in my name and in the name of my brother and my partner Esmeriz thank you once more for the very kind attention you have given our case.[8]

Then in January of 1931 a further technical development appeared to offer salvation; the first sound-film in Portuguese. 'A Severa', the story of Maria Severa and Count de Vimioso, was filmed at the Epinay studios in Paris during the winter of 1930/31, directed by the veteran Portuguese film-maker J. Leitão de Barros, and produced by J. Bernard Brunius and the French director René Clair. The lead role of Severa was given to a rising young Fadista on the Lisbon cafe circuit, Dina Teresa. Physically she resembled most of the popular images of Severa; plump and round-faced, of medium build with dark wavy hair. The Fados, specially written for the film by Marianna Alves and the Coimbra Fadista Paradella de Oliveira, were traditional in style and reflected the reverence that most Fadistas felt for Severa. It is interesting, however, to note that in the more cosmopolitan environment of Paris, a Coimbra and a Lisbon Fadista were able to collaborate in a way that they would almost certainly not have been able to do in Portugal.

The story, by Júlio Dantes, was to some degree reinterpreted. The plot includes another lover for Severa, a handsome but poor Fadista who vies with the Count for her favours. Eventually, she loses both men and dies, suddenly, of a combination of consumption and a broken heart, in mid-song. The tale had started life as a stage play, and versions of it ran on and off for years in the Lisbon theatres. It was then re-written as a novel by Dantes who in turn wrote the screenplay. The film was a huge success, not only in Portugal, but elsewhere in the Lusophone world. It ran to packed houses in Rio and São Paulo; it opened successfully in Portuguese communities across the United States; it eventually found its way to Lourenço Marques, Goa and Macao, and everywhere it played, the records – and the sheet music – followed. There were six songs from the film, released on three sequentially-numbered 78s. Because the technology to transfer performances from film to disc had not yet been fully developed, all six songs were re-recorded in HMV's Paris studio in early 1931. On 22 January Alfred Clark, of Gramco's head office, wrote to the affiliate in Paris, Compagnie Française du Gramophone:

> I have heard that the Portuguese Maestro Frederico de Freitas has already been in touch with you on the question of the recording from the Portuguese talking-film 'A Severa', and that you referred him to the Gramophone Company Ltd.
>
> I shall be very much obliged if you will now arrange an interview with this gentleman, who is now living at the following address:
>
> c/o M H Da Costa
> Rue St Martin 359
> Paris, 3e
>
> and work out the cost of recordings. I wish the expense kept as low as possible. When these figures are complete, please send them to me for my approval without delay. The recording can take place between January 28th and February 15th. I do not wish you, however, to make any arrangements for these sessions until the programme has been received and approved by me.[9]

In the event, Dina Teresa recorded two authentic Fados, 'Velho Fado de Severa' and 'Novo Fado de Severa' (Severa's old Fado and Severa's new Fado); three other supporting players from the film, Maria Sampaio, Maria Isabel and Sylvestre Alegrim, sang one song each and a small French orchestra contributed a side of incidental music. Offered by Gramco to GBDP as finished product on their own plum-coloured EQ series, they were welcome additions to Allen's Portuguese catalogue. He issued a separate four-page leaflet, advertising all three issues and featuring a lavish photo spread of stills from the film. However, simultaneous with this flurry of optimism, events were taking place in London that would end GBDP's days as the leading gramophone company in Portugal.

The major European recording companies, The Gramophone Company, Columbia (including Odeon and Parlophone) and Pathé had, throughout 1930, been in secret negotiations to merge their operations. Although the Wall Street crash and encroaching depression were not the root cause of these talks, they had the effect of creating a sense of urgency about the matter. By the spring of 1931 agreement had been reached and an announcement was made that Electric

Musical Industries Ltd (EMI) had been formed. This new company controlled the Columbia, HMV, Odeon, Parlophone, Pathé, Regal and Zonophone labels in every territory that each company had previously operated in. This meant that the one company virtually monopolized the gramophone and record markets of Europe, Africa, India and large tracts of the near, middle and far east. Only the London-based Decca company provided any serious competition, and then only in Britain and limited parts of Western Europe.

It also meant that a good deal of rationalization had to begin. Where each company had had an agent in a territory, competing on their behalf, only one was now necessary. In Portugal, this meant the first step towards the ultimate demise of GBDP and Mr Allen's increasingly grandiose plans. At first the newly formed EMI retained all three agents, GBDP, Carvalho and Ricardo Lemos, but changed some of the contractual terms. In an internal memo between S.H. Sheard and a Mr A.T. Lack at Hayes on 7 October 1932, Sheard noted:

> When I was in Lisbon and Oporto, I had conversations not only with the Grand Bazaar do Porto but also with Mr. Carvalho, the distributor for the Columbia Co. During these conversations I enquired as to how the dealers had accepted the reduction in their discount from 25% to 20% and was told by both parties that they had taken this reduction extremely well, it having been pointed out to them that the only real alternative would have been to increase the retail price, which everyone is anxious to avoid.
>
> You may remember that the question had to be considered owing to the considerable increase in the customs tarriff on our goods. Both distributors, however, made a very strong point of the urgent necessity of EMI requesting the Odeon distributors to fall into line in regard to their dealers.
>
> I was given an invoice showing that the Odeon distributor in Oporto, Ricardo Lemos was allowing up to 30% on one of the higher categories of Odeon records. There is no allegation of general price cutting or any wrong method of trading, against the Odeon distributors, but simply that a desire is expressed that they should be notified with regard to the necessity for trading on similar lines to those adopted by the Columbia distributor and our own.
>
> Both Mr. Carvalho and Mr. Allen are in agreement with regard to holding meetings from time to time on matters of mutual interest, but feel that a lead should be given first from Lindstroem [of Odeon] so that the Odeon distributors will realise that the movement has official sanction and approval.[10]

It seems clear that while everyone experienced some problems adjusting to the merger, Lemos had more than most. He was simply unable to understand that the Odeon label, for whom he had been an agent for over 25 years, had joined forces with the competition that he had fought so hard against. In 1936 Hayes granted GBDP an extension of its contract with them in a straightforward one-paragraph document:

> We hereby authorise you to import into Portugal goods manufactured or supplied by us, and also Trade Mark labels, plates, transfers and advertising material bearing our Trade Mark ('Dog & Gramophone' and the words 'His Master's Voice') supplied by us.[11]

but they offered them no new recording sessions. Instead, they made arrangements with Valentim de Carvalho to hold a new session, the first for five years, in Lisbon.

Developments in the late 1930s

The 1936 recording sessions that EMI undertook for Carvalho represented something of a renaissance in recorded Fado. The last new records anyone had had to sell were now five years old and, even in remote areas, they were becoming a little stale. This new batch of releases was intended to give Carvalho an edge over Grand Bazaar and, given the demise of Brunswick-Polydor, it virtually left them with a clear field. However, the initial releases did not sell as well as either EMI or Carvalho had expected. As late as summer 1938 they were still drawing upon masters from the 1936 recordings to present 'new' Fados to the public in an attempt to boost interest.

The slow progress of issuing these records, and the apparent lack of conformity when ordering product, produced some frustration at Hayes:

> When making out further copies of titles, please be very careful not to insert anything which is not to appear on the label.
>
> Sometimes on your labels with singers accompanied by instruments, you use the word 'accompanhamento', but on others you do not. We would like to know whether there is some particular reason for this or if you would always like it inserted.
>
> We now come to the question of all the remaining unissued Portuguese recordings. These we have listed on the attached schedules. You have had tests of all of them. You will see that some failed in wear tests and must be considered lost, since no satisfactory commercial recordings can be made from these. We shall be glad to hear from you in due course over what length of time you plan to issue these outstanding recordings, but in the meantime may we suggest that, of those numbers of which two recordings have been made, you indicate to us the ones which may be considered as cancelled.[12]

Carvalho continued to prevaricate but, despite the frustrations, Hayes continued to do the best it could to get Carvalho to issue the balance of the recordings:

> We note with pleasure that you are contemplating the issue of some of the 1936 recordings; in connection with [four of them], these were condemned because they developed faults after a few playings due to indifferent placing of the instrumentalists at the time of the recording:
>
> We note, however, that you are very interested in the four numbers, and as a further sign of our anxiety to give you every assistance we possibly can in your record trade, we passed the recordings over to our technical department to see whether, by re-recording, they could eliminate those patches in the records which were breaking down. The result attained is, in our opinion, satisfactory and samples will be sent to you by post.[13]

However, this cordiality masked a deeper level of frustration. In an internal memo from Mr Offord, of the Export Department at Hayes to a Mr Thomas, he noted:

> It might be of interest for you to have the facts on hand in connection with Carvalho's recordings in 1936. As you know there was a tremendous commotion about this recording, but sales have been disappointing.
>
> A summary of the position is as follows:
>
> A.   Recordings made 109
> B.   Good waxes processed (see note below)..138
> C.   Recordings issued and coupled 74

> D.   Sales to date, all markets, i.e. Portugal and outside (average 260) 9824
> E.   Recordings still to be issued 35

> You will note that the number of waxes processed is in excess of the recordings made. This is due to the fact that we had to process a large number of version (take) 2 when version 1 was perfectly OK, and, in addition, had to dub one or other when the order was placed.
>
> The sales of all territories have been taken in order to be perfectly fair to Carvalho. Of the numbers which have yet to be issued, we can probably rely on most of them having to be re-dubbed because the general complaint seems to be that all of them were too soft.
>
> Whilst you were on holiday, Carvalho wanted us to dub a whole lot of numbers but would not give an order. On Mr Duncan's instructions I wrote to him that we would do further dubbing against receipt of a firm order for 150 records. He replied to the effect that he could not possibly order 150 and we left the matter at that. He has just placed a recent order for 100 each of six of his recordings, one of which had to be dubbed.[14]

Despite all the complications, Hayes remained convinced that, so far as their business was concerned, Portugal was still a country with a worthwhile future. However, some decisions had to be made about who was going to represent them. Ignoring the deepening crisis in Europe, Hayes prepared a report on Portuguese territories in July 1939 which concluded that, while not ideal, Carvalho was doing the best he could under the circumstances and that both Hayes and Carvalho had faith in a better future. However, a letter from Grand Bazaar, received at the same time the report was being prepared, spread some alarm in the export department:

> This writer has now spent a few weeks in Lisbon studying the best way of developing, in future, the HMV business. We have received already some interesting suggestions but it has occurred, in the meantime, to our mind, that it would be perhaps more advantageous for the development of business and principally in what concerns the recreation of business to propose to our mutual friends Messrs Valentim de Carvalho an agreement with our firm by which we would be agreeable to consider the possibility of appointing them as our sub-agents for HMV products in the south of Portugal, on the condition that, reciprocating, they would be disposed to appoint our firm as their sub-agents in the north of Portugal. The writer has had in Lisbon a few interviews with Messrs Carvalho and we are all convinced that such an agreement, details of which are now being studied, will improve the business in Portugal, with considerable advantages to the Gramophone Cy & Columbia which is doing very small business in the North.
>
> We believe that you will see no inconvenience to this idea. from which appreciable benefits can be expected. We are sending today to Messrs Carvalho the basis we propose for the agreement and after receiving his answer and comments, we shall communicate with your good selves.[15]

They couldn't have been more wrong. Hayes replied, curtly:

> We have your letter of the 8th in which you suggest some reorganisation of the method of distribution of our products. Our feeling in this matter is that we have been in no way satisfied by the way in which you have handled our business during recent years, and as the question of the distribution of goods is in our hands, we have cabled to you on the 15th inst asking you to suspend any action in this matter, because we are carefully examining the whole situation and we propose to send a representative to Portugal in the very near future, for the purpose of investigating what should be done with regard to future distribution of our goods in your territory.[16]

Clearly furious at what it saw as interference, EMI sent a Mr Benning – an executive with fluent Portuguese – to see both Grand Bazaar and Carvalho. His instructions to them, that each firm would be responsible for selling all EMI product in its own clearly defined territory, were reflected in the somewhat hurt tones of a letter that Mr Allen sent to Hayes on 10 August:

> We note, with thanks, your information that you have decided to arrange the question of the distribution of your products in Portugal on the basis discussed here with Mr. Benning, in the past month of April when we had the pleasure of receiving his visit.
>
> Only with the purpose of showing you our condescendence and good will, facilitating the question, we accept the division as suggested by your goodselves, viz; the fortieth parallel of latitude, although, as we informed Mr. Benning we could expect to have on our side the whole area of Beira Baixa [a largely unpopulated plains area].
>
> To avoid possible future disappointments, we remind you here, once again, that we remain in control of a much smaller part of the country, which is also the poorest part and positively, the one which is much more affected by the crisis in the wine, cotton and other trades.
>
> As Mr. Benning informed that he is having now his holidays we must ask you to remind him, immediately upon his return, that we are anxious to receive complete information regarding this matter.
>
> With the delay occuring since we started discussing this question we have been losing many many opportunities and we hope now that you will be able to avoid, as much as possible, further delay.[17]

Benning remained unmoved by Allen's pleas and reiterated EMI's position; Grand Bazaar could sell all EMI goods north of the fortieth parallel – essentially from Coimbra up to the border – and nowhere else. Carvalho would have the much richer south. Benning's motives were clear. As instigators of the proposed subleasing deal between themselves and Carvalho, Grand Bazaar were being punished, but subtly so, since they had, in fact, been given the full range of EMI goods they originally wished to sell. Benning, however, was well aware that the shifting economics of Portugal had left Porto in crisis and moved the centre of wealth to Lisbon. By drawing a line at the fortieth parallel, EMI were isolating Grand Bazaar and making a choice that Carvalho would be the distributor for the future.

The Growth in Commercial Radio Broadcasting

In the meantime, the free-for-all situation in Portuguese radio broadcasting was about to change. Until at least 1930 nobody in the record industry had taken radio seriously enough to think about it as a source of income. Records were routinely being played on the air, but the general reaction of record executives was that that could only do some good in terms of exposure and certainly did little harm. By the mid-1930s comparative global sales figures were telling them a different story. In areas such as Argentina, where radio growth was rapid and the penetration of the home receiver market was deep, record sales were falling dramatically.

In Portugal, by 1935, there were eleven radio stations operating independently, five in Lisbon, four in Porto, and one each in Faro and Santarém. All of them used gramophone records on a daily basis and none of them paid any royalties to do so. The industry now felt it was time that they did. Lobbying of various government departments around the world began in order to change laws that would allow record companies to collect a royalty payment each time a piece of recorded music was broadcast. Some nations settled this issue more quickly than others; in Portugal it resulted in prolonged confrontation. By late 1938, however, the Council of the International Federation of the Phonographic Industry, an industry-centred self-help group, had convinced Salazar's government that levying a small charge on each record played on the air was good for international relations. It would 'legitimize' radio broadcasting and bring it into closer co-operation with the established home entertainment industry. It was also made clear that, since major record groups like EMI and Decca were also the manufacturers of radio receivers, the growth of radio could possibly be blunted by non-cooperation. The bill was duly made law in Portugal late in 1938.

The War Years

While these developments took place, the political situation in the rest of Europe moved deeper into crisis. Although Portugal stood in neutrality, and would continue to do so, the declaration of hostilities that the British prime minister Neville Chamberlain was forced to announce on 3 September 1939 brought much of EMI's pan-European activities to a halt. Engineers and British staff were recalled from Berlin, Vienna, Budapest, Prague, Milan, and, a few months later, during the blitzkrieg of spring 1940, from Brussels and Paris.

Offices in Greece, Turkey and Egypt remained open. Spain, still recovering from the civil war that had ended recording activities in 1936, was already considered a lost cause. Portugal, however, posed a different problem. In essence, there was no political reason why Portugal could not continue to be supplied. Indeed, given their new position, every effort had to be made to dissuade them from the fascist cause. However, the restructuring that EMI, and indeed, all other record companies, had to undergo rendered continuation of trade practically impossible. Skilled staff at the factories, from recording engineers to processing workers, were being called into the armed forces. A number were allowed to stay on a 'reserved occupation' status, on the basis that the manufacture of gramophone records was necessary for the morale of the country and for propaganda purposes. That did not include much room for export work. Despite this, and taking Portugal's neutrality into account, two sessions were held in Lisbon during the war years. The first, in March 1942, was specifically to record the rising young phenomenon Fernando Farinha, and the second, a larger session in the spring 1944, featured Maria Carmo de Torres and the legendary Alfredo Duarte, making his first appearance on record in fourteen years.

Nevertheless, the war did not hinder Portugal's film industry. Dr Salazar's inability to see the propaganda potential of film, as Hitler and Goebbels did, meant that it received neither funding nor interference from the government.

Salazar once remarked to director António Lopes Ribeiro that cinema was 'that terribly expensive industry' and he left film makers to their own devices.

As a result of Salazar's *laissez faire* policy Portuguese film briefly flourished, and the first half of the 1940s was something of a golden age for light musical comedy, producing films that have, over the years, become deeply loved favourites among the Portuguese. Taking a motif from the first sound film actually made in Portugal, the 1933 musical 'A Canção de Lisboa', the Ribeiro brothers, António Lopes and Francisco, produced a series of pictures of which António Lopes's 1941 production 'O Pai Tirano' (The Tyrannical Father) was the first. The father figure was suspiciously Salazaresque, and although viewed as a stern authoritarian, he emerged from the plot as a wise and loving parent who kept his family out of the trouble it would otherwise surely fall foul of. The message of the wisdom of benign dictatorship was very clear to a still-neutral Portugal.

The Ribeiros followed this modest success the next year with the immensely popular 'O Pátio das Cantigas' (Song of the Courtyards). Featuring Francisco Ribeiro himself, Laura Alves as the heroine, António Silva in the matinée-idol role, the well-loved comedian Vasco Santana (clearly influenced by Oliver Hardy) and his long-term partner Reginald Duarte, the plot was another paean to an idealized Portuguese life. Gathered around a square in the city, each living their own lives, is the modest, chaste flower seller (Alves), the quiet, handsome young man (Silva) and a motley cast of stock characters who all perform their individual set pieces. When Alves's father dies, she goes to the window to sing a heartfelt Fado. Santana and Duarte, ensconced in a wine cellar, are interrupted from their own Fado practice by an enthusiastic neighbour who insists on interrupting with applause until they give up. A glamorous and successful singer returns from Brazil to visit her home in the square, Santana provides comic relief with a wonderfully funny drunken routine and Dr Salazar is specifically referred to as Portugal's saviour by keeping the country out of the war. The hero and heroine, after the usual on-again off-again rituals, finally admit to being in love and a street festival is held at the climax. Emphasis is placed upon the importance of family and friends, the opportunities available in Brazil and the preservation of both neutrality and Portuguese culture. However, following the production of the less successful and rather dark film 'Aniki-Bóbó' the following year, the Ribeiro brothers went bankrupt in 1943. Only director Artur Duarte continued working within the light comedy genre, producing 'O Costa Da Castelo' (Costa of the Castle) in 1943 and 'A Menina Da Rádio' (The Radio Girl) in 1944. In comparison to 'O Pátio das Cantigas', however, Duarte's success was modest, and the history of Fado in Portuguese cinema was now destined to become a 'star system', the film being simply a vehicle for the singer.

By early 1944 there was enough confidence in the outcome of the war to generate dialogue between Carvalho and Hayes. Feeling his way towards an increasingly optimistic post-war future, Carvalho wrote:

We take the liberty of addressing you on the subject of publicity. It is a long time since we have been making the publicity of the Columbia and HMV trade marks and we receive from the referred companies an allowance of 1/3d. on the cost of the announcements published in the most important newspapers of our country.

Since we are gradually developing the propaganda of the Parlophone mark, principally due to the fact of the issue of the new Portuguese records under this mark, we now ask if you are in agreement to give us also an allowance on future advertisements and we would proceed towards yourselves as we have always done up to the present with other associates, sending you always the receipts of all payments made referring to publicity of your mark as well as the diaries [newspapers] where the same are inserted. You would send us in return the credit note for the allowance which would be established.[18]

A suggestion which was agreed to by Hayes; advertising in Lisbon's nightly *Diairio de Noticias* began the following month.

In the meantime Carvalho wasn't above a little deviousness:

I wish to inform you that some days ago Mr. Ricardo Lemos spoke of getting the representation of Decca. This should be a real calamity for the business in Portugal. Concerning this communication I write you to ask what do you think about the inclusion of the Decca representation for our firm.

The matter is perhaps out of our contract. But it seems of easy conception the convenience of leaving the Decca affairs of preference in our hands than seeing these treated by someone like Lemos.

Lemos is overcome, suffocated with records and he tries to get rid of them by all means. He is a very dangerous man under all points since he has not yet decided to change his process of working, the use of disrespecting contracts, prices and discounts. It has always been his way of acting and it always will be.[19]

It hardly seems feasible that Carvalho was unaware of Decca's total independence from, and rivalry with, EMI; rather, he seems to have taken a somewhat roundabout route to warning Hayes of Lemos's plans. In theory, Lemos was still an EMI agent, although he seemed to have done little business since 1939.

Ignoring Carvalho's pleas for the Decca contract – about which EMI could do nothing anyway – but probably quietly taking on board the information regarding Lemos, they replied:

To assist us in planning our production for the period immediately after the end of the war, we would be much obliged if you could let us have some idea of the quantity of acoustic gramophones, record players and needles you are likely to require during the first post-war year.

If you could see your way to placing a firm order now, it would ensure earliest possible delivery; but if you cannot do this, we would be glad to have a rough estimate of your probable requirements, which would not, of course, commit you in any way.[20]

Perhaps, as much as anything, EMI were encouraged by two resolutions passed at the May 1945 congress of Dr. Salazar's ruling National Union Party in Lisbon. The first stated:

The purpose of the new plan is to centralize and modernize industry with special attention to exportable products. Emphasis is laid upon the need for better industrial education and an improved standard of living for the workers. It is estimated that the first phase of this comprehensive plan could be accomplished in eight years at a cost of about £13,000,000.[21]

Which meant the likelihood of more disposable income among the Portuguese. The second stated:

> It is resolved to maintain, strengthen and develop the alliance with Britain, including the Dominion; to develop good relations with France, with particular reference to the defence of Western Europe; to strengthen links with Brazil; and to collaborate with the United States, recognising its geographical position within the Atlantic Square.[22]

Which meant that while Portugal was restating its adherence to 'the old alliance' with Britain, it was also officially courting countries – and economies – that could potentially compete in the new Portuguese market. Moreover, EMI's letter was a clear indication of how EMI saw the post-war future in Portugal. Grand Bazaar and Lemos received no such offers; indeed, a long plea for goods from Grand Bazaar, sent as late as August 1945, was simply ignored at Hayes. EMI's interests in Portugal would be best served by its proven ally, Carvalho. In a mood of ebullience and expectancy, Carvalho wrote:

> The latest days have been of the greatest joy for the Portuguese people who can at last show his feelings about the war, the allies and the ideal of liberty and human dignity, still forgotten in some countries. For the high deeds of the brave English people and for the next complete victory I send you advancedly my sincerest congratulations.
> With the next end of the war we have several matters to deal with regarding the future affairs of the EMI in Portugal. And I find it well that I go as soon as possible and talk to you, but I should like to do so when you may think it convenient. I ask you then to note my wish of visiting Hayes and get informed of the right occasion for that.[23]

However, with Japan remaining unconquered until August 1945, it was not until early 1946 that Carvalho arrived at Hayes. He came away with a re-negotiated contract, the details of which must have given him reason to smile. Clause one stated:

> The Gramophone Company hereby appoints Carvalho its sole distributor for acoustic gramophones, gramophone records, and accesories in Portugal, the islands of the Azores, Madeira, and Portuguese West Africa.[24]

It also allowed him most of the old contractual favours; an allowance for advertising, the supply of advertising material free of charge, continued freedom to arrange his own repertoire, a reimbursement of recording expenses, a 6% returns quota, a 60-day invoice settlement period with a generous £3000 ceiling and a 2½% cash discount for early settlement.

If Carvalho left Hayes a happy man, however, the same could not be said of J.E. Greville Perrit; as E. Perrit & Co., he ran a general import-export business from the East End of London that specialized in trading with Madeira. On 17 June 1946 he wrote to EMI:

> You will remember that we have been your sole agent in Madeira for over 20 years, working with our good friends J. S. Camacho & Co (in Madeira), who visit us every year.
> We only relinquished the business in the war years because of the regulations that records could only be sent by the makers direct, but we now wish to resume our old and pleasant relationship.
> We enclose an order and shall be glad to know when these goods will be ready.[25]

EMI's overseas department replied two days later:

> We very much regret that we are not able to execute your order which is returned herewith.
>   Would you be good enough to advise Mssrs Camacho to get in touch with our distributor in Portugal, Mr Valentim de Carvalho, of Lisbon.[26]

A near-apoplectic reply was received at Hayes ten days later:

> Madeira is not part of Portugal and it is geographically wrong to put Madeira under Portugal. Madeira is always in close touch with London, letters and ships taking normally 3½ days, whereas via Lisbon the time is nearer three months.
>   Besides, WE started this business, 20 years ago, and we wish to continue it, and Mr Camacho wishes to continue it through us.
>   We think it most extraordinary that you should wish to cut out a British firm in favour of a foreign agent, who is not well placed for doing business anyway, especially as we started it, and have been doing it all along.
>   Please be good enough to report on our order and let us know when you can deliver.[27]

In replying on 4 July, Hayes dug its heels in:

> We have carefully noted your remarks with reference to the transfer of the control of our business in Madeira to our distributors in Portugal, but regret that we cannot see our way to alter our decision in this matter. Post-war conditions have entailed a considerable reorganisation of our set-up overseas in the effort to secure the greatest possible development of our export business. We would point out that our turnover for Madeira has never been as large as we consider possible for this market, and we consider that Mr Valentim de Carvalho, who is more aware of the potentials of this market than we are, will be better able to develop our business there.
>   The writer has just returned from a visit to Lisbon and while there discussed the question of Mssrs Camacho & Co., with Mr Carvalho, and we do not doubt that we will be able to make arrangements with Camacho that will be agreeable to them.[28]

Still furious and clearly hurt, Perritt replied:

> We have been 50 years at this address and we have always found the formation of big combines resulting in the British Merchant losing the business. We used to do an enormous trade in explosives with people like Curtis & Harvey, E.C. Powder Co, Nobels, Kynosh, and others, but when all these firms became amalgamated into Explosives Trade Ltd they refused to sell to British Merchants.
>   It looks as though there would be nemesis overtaking these large amalgamations, for instance the ICI is going to be taken over by the Socialist Government and nationalised, and probably the Gramophone Co will follow suit, in view of its connection with wireless and television. This would appear to be the penalty for greatness as the government will never bother to nationalise a large number of small firms, but when they become colossal like ICI it becomes easy to nationalise them.
>   It does seem to us very unpatriotic for big manufacturers in this country to seek to eliminate the British Merchants who originally were instrumental in getting them the business, especially where WE can get the business and the foreign agent cannot, as in this case.
>   We trust that you will reconsider the whole matter and that you will execute the enclosed orders.[29]

It was, however, a lost cause. EMI steadfastly refused to give Madeira back to Perritt and, following further acrimonious exchanges, the correspondence ceased.

Carvalho was not completely without competition. English Decca had launched a Portuguese series in late 1944, signing the popular Hermina Silva to its roster, but despite Decca's excellent sound quality recordings and pressings, the series was not a success, and it folded after less than two years. More successful was the Porto-based Rádio Triunfo Company, whose 'Melodia' label was doing brisk business with local recordings and re-releases of masters from the Brazilian 'Continental' label. That these included the first recordings of Amália Rodrigues, possibly the biggest selling records ever released in Portugal to that date, caused some measure of concern at Carvalho's, especially since he was unable even to offer them for sale in his own retail stores.

Carvalho's 1945 and 1946 catalogues reflect a wide cross section of not only styles – Fado, 'folklorico', instrumental and popular – but also of vintage. Recordings up to 20 years old were still being offered. In the case of António Menano and Edmundo de Bettencourt this reflected steady sales, as evidenced by surviving pressing orders from 1945 that list them, but others, like the 1926 João do Carmo records or José Porfírio's solitary 1929 release, deleted in 1939, were probably listed because they were slow sellers and still in stock. What was missing from Carvalho's catalogues was the new material on Melodia.

These new records were also being played on the now nationally established radio network. The state-owned Emissora Nacional, with three major relay stations, could be heard all across Portugal by 1947. Although controlled by Salazar's government, who certainly filtered news to some degree, it was nothing like as heavy handed as the Brazilian government's interference with the nightly 'Hour of Brazil' propaganda programme broadcast on every station simultaneously.

Radio's Electro Mechanico, Peninsular and Renascença, independent Portuguese-owned stations, could be heard in the Lisbon and Porto areas, and Porto listeners also had the Rádio Club de Portugal (a non-profit broadcasting collective) to tune to. Between them these stations broadcast an average of nine Fado shows a day, featuring a mixture of live performances and recordings. The details of these shows could be found in the weekly magazine *Rádio Mundial*, which listed the times and details of every station's programmes, and supplied feature articles and photos of radio personalities. Its 1947 readers poll of favourite stars is revealing not only for the listener's loyalty to Portuguese artists, but also for the popularity of other cultures:

1. Amália Rodrigues
2. Maria Clara
3. Bing Crosby
4. Alberto Ribeiro
5. Maria da Graça
6. Jean Sablon (French)
7. Frank Sinatra
8. Dick Haymes (American)

9. Francisco Canaro (Argentine)
10. Rosita Serrano (Spanish)
11. Maria Gabriella
12. Herminia Silva
13. Imperio Argentina (Spanish)
14. Charles Trenet (French)
15. Georges Boulanger (French)

A basic radio receiver was affordable, even for a modest Portuguese household, and once purchased, needed no further investment in the way that a gramophone did. It brought news, features, plays, music and companionship to its listeners and, given the late development of television – which was not launched until 1956 – it remained a staple diet of entertainment for the Portuguese.

Carvalho's sales figures for 1947 and 1948 averaged 27,500 per annum. Given this volume, and the duty charged upon records by the Portuguese customs, EMI started to have thoughts, as early as May 1949, about setting up a record-pressing plant in Portugal; it would be their first one in the country, and would allow records to be manufactured more cost effectively.

Some people at Hayes, largely accountants, were unhappy about this. They suspected that if a pressing plant were set up in Lisbon under Carvalho's control he might use it to manufacture other companies' discs as well as EMI. One person noted:

> The trouble with the Portuguese business is that the agent is quite happy earning a large margin of profit on a small business, and is not prepared to expend in expanding it. In any case, if we put a plant there, even if Carvalho pays for it, we should not permit him to press or make any other recordings.[30]

The matter rested for almost three years but, following further cajoling on Carvalho's part, EMI sent Mr Benning to Lisbon to negotiate a deal with Carvalho. As a result, a new contract was issued, consolidating all the EMI-owned trademarks (HMV, Columbia and Parlophone) and allowing Carvalho sole distributorship of all three. A simple pressing plant was to be established just outside Lisbon that could manufacture 10" 78rpm discs from metal stampers supplied by EMI facilities in France. A retail price equivalent to 4/6d was fixed, with EMI receiving 3d per pressing as a royalty. All expenses involved in setting up and running the plant would be borne by Carvalho but the expertise and equipment would be supplied by EMI, including the training of personnel to run the operation. Matrices would cost Carvalho 20% above the cost of manufacture and a target of 60,000 pressings per annum was agreed. By 1953 this simple plant was supposed to have been operational.

Both Carvalho and the Overseas Department at Hayes knew this was necessary, as Melodia was pressing large quantities of records in Porto, and they had to be challenged or, it was felt, EMI and Carvalho would start to lose ground. It was, however, a slow process. An internal memo at EMI summed up the situation:

> In December 1953, two sets of agreements were made with Valentim de Carvalho, in the names of the English mark owning companies: one set referred to distribution, the other to the terms on which Mssrs Carvalho would be allowed to press records in Portugal.

The pressing fees payable by Mssrs Carvalho were established at 5d. per 78rpm record for international repertoire and 3d. per record for local recordings, with a minimum of £600 in the first year of operation, £675 in the second year and £750 in any subsequent year.

Although 1954 should have presumably been the first year of operation, in practice actual manufacture did not begin until January 1956. Accruals of pressing fees in 1956 were approximately £700. At the request of Mssrs Carvalho we agreed, in early 1957, to waive our claim to any pressing fees for 1954 and 1955, while in respect of 1957 we agreed to a minimum of £675, the guaranteed minimum of £750 per year being applicable for the year 1958 and onwards. In 1957, accruals were slightly more than £750. In 1958, local production of records has been less than anticipated due to the collapse of the 78rpm market and delays in commencement of local 45rpm manufacture. As a consequence, pressing fee accruals up to the end of September amount to approximately £304 only, and accruals for the year will probably not be much in excess of £500.[31]

Thus, by the time the plant was fully operational it was close to being outmoded and, furthermore, Carvalho had a number of small local labels to compete with, the most active of which was right on his doorstep. Manoel Simões, owner of a record shop on the Rua do Carmo, just a few streets from Carvalho's premises, had started the 'Estoril' record label sometime around 1952. Within a short space of time Simões had amassed a large and interesting selection of music. His 1956 catalogue listed more than three hundred 78s, over half of which were also available on the new 45rpm format. He also offered 30 long-playing albums. His prices were competitive, at 37½ escudos for 78s and 55 escudos for 45s; his pressings, made in Porto – probably by Rádio Triunfo – were excellent quality and his roster of artists impressive. He had signed, among many others, the legendary Alfredo Duarte, the immensely bankable Fernando Farinha and the increasingly popular Argentina Santos. His success made some heavy inroads into Carvalho's local business, especially the emerging tourist industry, but Simões could not compete with him either nationally or in the territories. Around 1960 the Estoril label was forced to suspend its operations due to what was described as 'incorrect accounting' submitted by Simões to SECTP, the Portuguese composers' society. From that point on, Simoes contented himself making custom pressings for local companies and running his record shop, Casa Amália, where at the time of this book's publication, he can still be found.

The Italian company Fonit joined the Portuguese market briefly in about 1958, as did the obscure Rouxinol and Rapsódia labels, both probably pressed by Rádio Triunfo, but none made much impact. By that year the only serious contenders were Carvalho, Alvarado (Rádio Triunfo's replacement for Melodia), and Arnaldo Trindade's Porto-based Orfeão label.

Valentim de Carvalho himself had died in 1957. Although transfer of business to his nephew Rui and niece Maria Graça had begun a year or so earlier, his death caused some disruption in the business and may well have been a major contributory factor to the delay in opening the pressing plant. By 1959 the 78rpm record had been almost completely replaced by the two microgroove formats, 45rpm and LP. Most LPs were being issued in 10" diameter at this time; Amália Rodrigues, her sister Celeste, Maria Clara, Max, and other popular artists all featured on the new format. EMI allowed Carvalho to extend its overseas territory in 1959 to include Mozambique and Portuguese Goa. This was perhaps a little late in the day to be expanding into colonial territories, but it was felt at Hayes that, since Rui and Maria Graça Carvalho had requested them, and since there was no currently active business in either area, it could do no harm.

The Portuguese Record Trade in the 1960s

By 1960 the situation in the Portuguese record trade had altered considerably from the heady days of 1946. Much of the activity was neatly summed up in a report made by G.C. Alexander, of EMI's export department, following his visit to Portugal in April of that year:

> The Carvalhos estimate that they do 40% of the record business in the country, followed by Deutsch Gramofon Gesselschaft with 15%, RCA with 12%, Phillips with 10% and Rádio Triunfo (whose production is mainly local repertoire under the Alvarado trade mark) with 8%.
>
> There are approximately 500 record dealers in Portugal, but the great majority of these are in a very small way of business, and the number of really effective and well-organised retailers is probably not much more than fifty.
>
> In view of the low standard of living of the great majority of the population, the level of record sales per capita is much lower than in other countries of Western Europe.
>
> There are virtually no working class consumers of records, nor is the teenage market at all important. The main consumers are the middle and upper classes, with a considerable contribution being made by the tourist trade, especially in the Lisbon and Estoril areas.
>
> Sales of 78rpm records have virtually ceased – I saw them being jobbed off at cut prices in a few shops. The pop market consists very largely of EPs, the proportion of 45rpm singles having fallen very sharply in the last couple of years. The LP market is mainly for classical music. The Carvalhos said that 80% of their sales consist of 45rpm records – mostly EPs – 13% classical LPs, 4% pop LPs and 3% 78rpms.
>
> In the pop field, the interest is mainly for local recordings (Fados in the Lisbon area, folk music in the north and provinces, and a small amount of local dance music), closely followed by repertoire of Latin-American Italian, Spanish, French and US origin, more or less in that order. The demand for Brazilian records was very much in evidence.
>
> Pop music, including Fados, is broadcast on records from morning to night by half a dozen stations in the Lisbon area, supplemented by a further network of stations in the provinces. Frequently, neither titles nor artists are announced so the value of this exposure is dubious, although Carvalho and other leading firms buy air time to promote their new releases.
>
> Conditions in the record business generally have been very unhealthy for the past couple of years. This is largely the result of the excessive importation of records from Germany, Holland, France, the USA and elsewhere. The flooding of the market with these records has led to the supplying of records on consignment. The lead given by importing firms has been followed by Rádio Triunfo with that firm's local product Alvarado.
>
> I was able to see for myself that many small tobacconists, stationers and similar retail shops had a rack or basket of records on display, the contents being mainly from the firms mentioned. I did not see any of the marks handled by Carvalho in these locations. I was told by Carvalhos that their competitors have given ridiculously high discounts and bonuses to the regular dealers, also very extended credit terms. One of the results of

this policy has been more or less open price cutting and the giving of rebates to retail customers.

Another unhealthy development during the past couple of years has been the establishment of an excessive number of dealers: while the purchase of initial stocks doubtless helped wholesale turnover, the entry into the field of many retailers without previous experience of the trade has resulted in the piling up of unsaleable stocks and a consequent reaction. Both in Lisbon and Oporto I heard of the considerable financial difficulties of many of even the largest dealers. The direct imports by all and sundry from the U.S.A. have also contributed towards the chaotic conditions.[32]

However, although Alexander was unhappy about general conditions, his views on Carvalho were more positive:

Since the death of Valentim de Carvalho in 1957, the conduct of the business has largely been the responsibility of Rui and Maria Graça de Carvalho, his nephew and niece. The Oporto branch is run by a brother-in-law Mr. Vasconcellos.

The Lisbon premises, though admirably located for retail purposes and undoubtedly the best record shop in town, are less suitable for wholesale work. The storerooms, workshops and offices are over-crowded. The Oporto premises are more impressive; modern and spacious.

Both in Lisbon and Oporto the Carvalhos are handling a wide range of products including (apart from records, reproducers and radio gramophones) such articles as radio television receivers, vacuum cleaners, refrigerators, floor polishers and other household appliances, pianos, cash registers and typewriters. They are beginning to realise that they are handling too many products. It is likely that they will give up television in the near future because of intense competition from GEC and German firms. I suggested to them that several of the other lines could also be eliminated so that more floor space could be devoted to records.

The employees in charge of the respective record departments (Mr. Cunha in Lisbon in particular) seemed to know their job very well. Mr. Pousal, in charge of advertising and promotion, who has excellent radio contacts, also made a favourable impression. I was very impressed and surprised by Carvalho's wholesale activities; they maintain nine travellers, four of whom work only with records. Lisbon and Oporto dealers are visited at least once a week, and country dealers once every six weeks or so. None of the competition firms operate so efficiently.

Both Rui and Maria Graça de Carvalho are intelligent and hardworking, and realise that there is a lot of room for improvement in their organisation, also that it will be essential for them to delegate more responsibility so that they can properly cope with the burden placed on them by the death of their uncle.[33]

Throughout the 1960s and 70s, the market remained largely stable and the Extended Play (EP) record outsold every other format. Although the same size and speed as a 45rpm single, it had the added advantages of carrying generally four songs rather than two, and was also packaged in a handsome cover, in the same way as a long-playing record. These covers would often feature a colour photo of the artist on the front and a variety of information on the back, from notes about the artist or the music, to details of who played the instruments and advertisements for other EPs. It also allowed a measure of flexibility, and some EPs contained three songs, two on one side and a third, much longer, on the other. The format was used, by Orfeu, to introduce new artists. Its regularly issued 'Sempre de Fado' series featured one song each by four different Fadistas; if the reaction to a specific singer was good, they would then graduate to their own record. The public liked EPs for a variety of reasons, but the main one was price. There was still a lot of resistance to buying any other format because it was considered to be too expensive. On the one hand LPs simply cost too much, on the other, single 45s were not regarded as being good value. The growing tourist industry also boosted sales of these appealing little records.

Carvalho, now operating its EMI contract solely under the Columbia logo, was also, by at least 1964, manufacturing and distributing a relaunched Decca label. The details of how they arranged this are vague, for Decca archives appear to have been lost and no mention of the matter surfaces in any EMI correspondence. Whatever anyone at either British firm may have felt about the situation, it made Carvalho the single biggest record distributor in Portugal. When the British pop music revolution of the 1960s filtered into Portugal, Carvalho had access to the two major catalogues. They were probably the only agent in the world to legitimately distribute records by both the Beatles and the Rolling Stones.

Carvalho competed in the Fado market with Rádio Triunfo's Alvarado label, the newly-established Orfeão and a selection of smaller operations including Carabine, pressed in France, Celta, manufactured in Spain, and local product on the Ff and Imavox labels. The few 45rpm singles that were issued often featured colour covers, to compete with the EP. Thus, Carlos Zel's 1978 hit 'Contrabandistas' featured a colour photo of a shop window full of illicit electrical appliances.

Later Developments

By the mid-1980s the Portuguese music industry was healthier than it had ever been. Still lagging a long way behind other European countries in overall sales, it was nevertheless considered buoyant in a 1981 American Billboard report and, during this essentially stable period, the sales of long-playing records overtook EP sales for the first time. In 1987 most Lisbon record shops featured large selections of vinyl LP records and cassette tapes. The cassette tape allowed greater flexibility for the producing company, since it was cheaper to manufacture in small quantities and, as a result, was used for the promotion of local artists in both Lisbon and Porto. Often, a resident singer in a Fado House would have a custom-made tape available for sale on the premises; many of these were aimed at the growing tourist trade and tended towards a homogeneous, blander style. Nevertheless, some were excellent and artists like Argentina Santos, whose main income always derived from running her own restaurant, routinely offered new songs on cassette.

At 5am on Friday, 26 August 1988, a fire broke out in Grandela, the historic art-deco department store in the heart of Lisbon's ancient Chiado area. In the six hours that it took to bring it under control, it had killed two people, injured 30 more, destroyed dozens of ancient and historic buildings, including a seventeenth-century jewellery shop, and razed the entire premises of Valentim de Carvalho.

Lost was not only stock but irreplaceable historical items; Amália Rodrigues's manager, João Belchor Veigas, worked out of the premises and his entire collection of files relating to her career since 1939 were incinerated. Also destroyed was the archive, a large collection of original sheet music, catalogues and records, both 78s and vinyl, which the company were just beginning to use to create historical reissues with. They had already compiled two albums by António Menano, one by Edmundo de Bettencourt and were planning more when the disaster struck. The loss was staggering – over 2000 people were rendered jobless overnight, the area was completely gutted and Lisbon went into shock.

Carvalho survived, however, and relocated in the Roçio area, in the main square, close to the railway station. Their new premises, modelled on the American Tower Stores pattern, is bright, clean and efficient. It in no way replaces the atmospheric antiquity of Rua Nova da Almada, Carvalho's home for 164 years, but the company still flourishes and today is again actively issuing Fados, both contemporary and vintage, on compact disc. Mario Simões continues to operate his small record shop, and a handfull of other independent retailers offer cassettes, CDs and videos in the Lisbon area. More than any other single company, however, the history of Valentim de Carvalho has been the history of recorded Fado.

Notes

1. Internal Gramco memo from Bruxelles office to London office, 3.13.04/EMI Archives.
2. Alfred Clark at Hayes to the Paris office, 3.3.26/EMI Archives.
3. Paris to Hayes, Feb. 1926/EMI.
4. Grand Bazaar Do Porto to Hayes, 8.6.29/EMI.
5. Grand Bazaar Do Port to Hayes, Feb. 1930/EMI.
6. Grand Bazaar Do Porto to Hayes, 4.27.30/EMI.
7. Sheard to Grand Bazaar Do Porto/EMI.
8. GBDP to Hayes, Aug. 36/EMI.
9. Alfred Clark to Paris office, 1.22.31/EMI.
10. Sheard to Lack, EMI internal memo, 7/10/32/EMI.
11. GBDP to Hayes, Aug. 36/EMI.
12. Hayes to Carvalho, 5.30.38/EMI.
13. Hayes to Carvalho, 7.13.38/EMI
14. EMI international memo, 8.12.38/EMI.
15. GBDP to Hayes, 1939/EMI.
16. GBDP to Hayes, 10.39/EMI.
17. GBDP to Hayes, 1939/EMI.
18. Carvalho to EMI, Feb. 1944/EMI.
19. Carvalho to EMI, 15.2.44/EMI.
20. EMI to Carvalho, 18.7.44/EMI.
21. Philip Graves (1945), *A Record of the War*, London: Hutchinson & Co.
22. Ibid.
23. Carvalho to EMI, 6.9.44/EMI.
24. Carvalho's 1946 contract/EMI.

25.   J.E. Perritt to EMI, 17.6.46/EMI.
26.   EMI to Perritt, 19.6.46/EMI.
27.   Perritt to EMI, 27.6.46/EMI.
28.   EMI to Perritt, 4.7.46/EMI.
29.   Perritt to EMI, 8.8.46/EMI.
30.   EMI internal memo, 16.7.49/EMI.
31.   EMI internal memo, 23.10.58/EMI.
32.   G.C. Alexander's report, April 1960/EMI.
33.   Ibid.

6 The Diaspora

Portugal founded its empire by maritime endeavour, and whatever anyone may choose to believe about the origins of the Fado, there is no doubt that Portuguese sailors and immigrants took it with them wherever they went. By the time the Fado had settled into a recognizable format, the Portuguese were routinely visiting the Americas, and their colonies in Madeira, the Azores, Macao, Goa, East Timor, São Tomé, Cape Verde, Angola, Mozambique and Guinea were established and thriving. They also traded extensively with mainland China, Japan, Hawaii and most of the rest of Europe, especially Britain and Germany.

Fado in the United States

By the first decade of the twentieth century there were small but significant Portuguese communities settling into North America, specifically in Massachusetts at Cambridge, Fall River and New Bedford, in Rhode Island at Providence, in New Jersey at Newark, in Washington State at Seattle and in California at Artesia, Chino, Martinez, Oakland, Richmond, San Diego, San José, San Leandro, Tulare and Visalia. The immigrants were not always from the mainland. Some came directly from Madeira or the Azores, and had never set foot in Portugal, but in the melting pot of early twentieth-century America, they were all regarded as Portuguese, especially by record executives hungry for the immigrant dollar.

From the beginning, record companies in the United States set out to cater to the musical tastes of every conceivable ethnic group. The Victor company's trade journal *The Voice of Victor* devoted space on a monthly basis to this aspect of the trade, exhorting their dealers to identify which ethnic groups were in their area and offering them catalogues, posters and streamers to attract their customers' attention. The magazine also offered useful demographics; in a 1912 article entitled 'Here's Where They Live!', which provided detailed statistical information on immigrant settlements around the country, Victor identified 67,453 'foreign-born' Portuguese and a further 134,318 using 'the mother tongue of the foreign stock'.[1] For the next decade it routinely ran advice-laden articles with titles such as 'How Do Your Reach Your Foreign Trade?', 'Do You Sell To Your Italians?', 'Polish Record Business is Increasing', 'Getting The Cream of Foreign Record Business' and 'Melting Pot Of The World is a Giant Market for Foreign Records'.

> Most of your customers are attracted to a Victrola because they hear on it music which they like and understand. Alien customers are attracted to it because they may hear on it songs in their own tongue, and dances in the style of their homeland. When you introduce a Victrola into one of these homes, you are also interesting the younger generation, whose taste covers a wider range of domestic selections. The following suggestions and comments come from successful foreign dealers and should be carefully considered by the dealer who is going after the foreign trade.
>
> Don't be deceived by appearances. Nearly every day a 'foreigner' enters some store and pays spot cash for a Victrola and records.
>
> Practise courtesy. The foreign language customer knows and appreciates this quality, and, in most cases, demands it before he is sold [goods]. A salesman or salesgirl who speaks other languages is an asset to your business. Customers like to be greeted in their own tongue, and enjoy talking over their record selections with someone who is in sympathy with them.
>
> A special demonstration room containing foreign hangers and catalogues is often convenient. It should be just as good as any other room in your store, and the Victrola on which the records are demonstrated should be in the best condition. Your foreign language customer knows music and is a severe critic.
>
> If there are foreign newspapers which have a local circulation, advertise in them. They reach people who cannot be reached in any other way.
>
> A foreign mailing list can be built up by obtaining names of memberships of Lodges, Churches, Beneficial Societies, et cetera. Newspaper coupon advertising, offering souvenirs, is often effective.
>
> Classify your mailing list, so that customers who buy records in German, Italian, Jewish, Polish, et cetera, receive monthly supplements regularly in their own language.
>
> In your monthly free trade service you receive two monthly foreign hangers; display them. Wholesalers will supply you with special foreign hangers, catalogues and supplements; display the hangers for ready reference and distribute the catalogues and supplements so that they count.
>
> Build up your stocks of foreign records, bearing in mind that in many languages the instrumental outsells the vocal. Victor national foreign advertising is driving customers in to you; each advertisement features new monthly records and some of the old ones. Insist on hearing the foreign samples when your wholesaler calls. When the sale of the Victrola is concluded, make the buyer a regular record customer. He will tell his friends and make other customers.
>
> Many wholesalers maintain foreign record specialists who are glad to assist the dealer; The Victor Company maintains a special Foreign Record Department which is always glad to furnish immediate information to the trade. Its services are at your command! Use them![2]

In 1910 Victor had recorded Mário Pinheiro, almost certainly a Brazilian, in New York. Accompanied by his own guitarra, he sang over 130 songs in a 12-day period, including Modinhas, Lundums and several Fados. Current research indicates that he was the first Lusophone artist to record in North America. Six years later, Victor started recording Manoel J. Carvalho, not so much a Fadista as an interpreter of all manner of Portuguese songs. He remained immensely popular throughout the 1920s:

Manoel Carvalho, whose rich baritone voice is heard on many Victor Portuguese records, was born on the island of São Miguel, one of the beautiful Azore islands, which belong to Portugal. As a boy of ten years, this singer gained recognition in a church choir. He was placed under the guidance of a competent teacher, and from that time to the present, the artist's vocal studies have continued. He has made several concert tours of this country, finding time in between to compose some good Portuguese songs. In record No.72532 Mr Carvalho has rendered two tuneful Fados in splendid style, with the accompaniment of the famous International Orchestra.[3]

By 1923 Victor found themselves competing with Columbia for every one of the 59 separately identified and targeted immigrant groups. Until 1926 both companies recorded local Portuguese musicians in their own studios on the East Coast, and during these first three years Columbia issued only 24 Portuguese records. However, from 1926, with the ability to offer the public the new Lisbon-recorded material from its London-based parent company, they took the lead in the Portuguese field. Between 1926 and 1933 they released material by Adelina Fernandes, Estevão Amarante, Dr António Menano, João do Carmo, Maria Emelia Ferreira, Dr Lucas Junot, Dr Edmundo de Bettencourt, Ermelinda Vitoria, José Porfirio and others, directly drawn from the Valentim de Carvalho recordings.

Victor was able to respond from about the middle of 1927, by issuing material from the newly instigated Grand Bazaar/HMV catalogue. They too were able to offer Adelina Fernandes, and also chose to release couplings by Artur Paredes, Paradella de Oliveira, Maria Silva, Armandinho, Madalena de Mello, Armando Goes, and José Dias as well as non-Fado material by the Foz Melody Band, the actor Chaby Pinheiro and singer Geraldo de Magalhaes. All these new issues bore the legend 'Recorded In Europe' on the label. Three years previously, Victor had exhorted their dealers to be aware of the important sales potential of this phrase:

> We Americans have an exotic taste; we like the things which have originated in and are brought here from foreign lands. This taste for exotics manifests itself in the boy who is making his first postage-stamp collection, as well as the millionaire collector of rare porcelains. It is a pardonable instinct, and one that is very easy for the Victor dealer to capitalise upon.
>
> Not every dealer or salesman is aware of the fact that over four thousand records in the present Victor foreign catalogues have been recorded in foreign countries, and at least two thousand in Europe. The foreign-born resident who is always seeking a connecting link with the home country will invariably find it in the Victor catalogue of his particular language.
>
> Until recently, there has been no special exploitation of these foreign recordings. During the past year, however, new record issues of European recordings bear the phrase 'Recorded In Europe'. This gives the salesman a distinct talking point in demonstrating his records to his customers.[4]

The New York-based *Phonographic Monthly Review*, the only contemporary journal to take note of foreign-language record issues as they appeared, offered sporadic commentary on Portuguese issues:

> The outstanding disk this month is Victor 81472 by Artur Paredes, of his own 'Variations in A Minor' and 'Fantasia'. Paredes is also heard on 81701 coupled with

Paradella De Oliveira ... Adelina Fernandes sings well on 81700 ... Columbia offers songs by Leonor Marques and Luís Eloy Da Silva ... There are three releases this month from Columbia, the best of which is the disk of original guitar solos by Dr. Afonso de Sousa ... Columbia and Victor are alone in this field, the former with vocals by António Menano and Estevão Amarante and the latter with six ten-inch disks and a feature 12-inch, the latter coupling selections by Corinna Freire and Adelina Fernandes.[5]

All this competitive activity was seriously curtailed by the depression that followed the stock market collapse of 1929. By 1932 Columbia, Victor and every other record company still solvent had drastically cut back all but their most popular, mainstream works. The catalogues of Albanian, Polish, Greek, Turkish, Italian and Portuguese records disappeared along with vast quantities of jazz, blues, country and cajun.

Throughout the 1930s the Library of Congress, in Washington DC, had undertaken an extensive field recording programme in order to document the life of the American people for civic posterity. This included photographing and making sound recordings of many communities, both urban and rural, from a wide variety of ethnic backgrounds. In 1938 and again in 1939 Sidney Robertson Cowell, a Library of Congress researcher, visited Oakland and Richmond, two towns in the Bay Area of Northern California. Among other ethnic groups of European origin, he found two Portuguese settlements, and recorded the music of several musicians, principally Alberto Mendes, Clifford Franks, Mr & Mrs Manoel Lemos and Mrs Alice Lemos Avila. Cowell's field notes, written as comments against numbered recordings, survive:

35MA3; Fragments from a Portuguese broadcast over KROW in Oakland: recordings made in Coimbra, according to Mr. Mendes.
35MB1; Fado accompaniment played by Mr.Lemos and Mr. Mendes on Portuguese violas. As played on the island of San Miguel (Azores).
37MB1; Fado accompaniment. Played by Mr Lemos and Mr. Mendes on the Portuguese violas (*sic*). As played on the island on San Miguel.
37MB2; Chamarrita. Most popular Portuguese song in California.
38MA1; Fado Portuguese (minor). From San Jorge.
38MA2; Fado Portuguese (corrido). Characteristic rhythm of Fado over which verses are improvised. These verses are however traditional and usually used to begin a Fado.
44MA1; 'Mariana Costureira', a song sung by Mrs. Avila, accompanying herself on the Portuguese guitar. Well known to all Portuguese in California.
38MA1 Choradinho. Sung for the Portuguese Minister to Washington about 1935, at his request, when he visited San Francisco. He knew the song as a boy.
A8MB1 Fado Hilario; Sung by Mrs. Avila, accompanying herself on the guitarra.
46MA1 Fado; Minha Mae e Pobrasinha (My mother is very poor). Sung by Mrs Avila accompanying herself on the guitarra. A Fado well known to all Portuguese in California.[6]

Cowell's notes are not always accurate in their description of instruments; often, a 'viola' was in reality a guitarra. What is especially interesting about these recordings, however, is that the performers were also absorbing songs from their new environment. Alongside the traditional Portuguese tunes they performed a Mexican corrido, a Neapolitan love song and a Spanish Jota.

The community in which the people surveyed by Cowell lived was served by radio station KROW based in Oakland, which daily broadcast a one-hour Portuguese-language programme heard throughout the Bay Area. In April 1942 Russell Lee, a photographer on assignment for the Library of Congress, visited the station and photographed the activities of those Portuguese-Americans involved in broadcasting the show. With war recently declared by Roosevelt, there was no question of maintaining neutrality; ignoring the politics of their homeland, Portuguese-Americans threw themselves into the war drive as enthusiastically as everyone else did. Russell Lee noted:

> Their programmes have gained new importance in the last few months as they strive to keep the Portuguese people of the section well-informed [sic]. They have also participated in many drives for the Red Cross, USO, War Bonds and stamps. Miss Sumares says 'I like all sorts of songs, both American and Portuguese. The Portuguese are singing people and we have all had many things to sing about and be happy about in this country.[7]

Little commercial recording activity is evident in the post-war years. Columbia sporadically issued a few Lisbon-made recordings from 1945 until 1952. The Oakland-based Anthony Sears label, Alto Mar records, operated from New York, and a small San Diego-based operation called Silvox appear to have been active at about the same time, but they issued less than a dozen records between them. Portuguese communities, however, seem to have had no trouble obtaining records directly from either Portugal or Brazil. Evidence suggests that a private importation network, operated principally by seamen on a community level, satisfied the local demands and precluded the necessity for domestic recording activity.[8]

*   *   *

California has remained, to this day, a favourite area for Portuguese immigrants. In San Leandro, the Portuguese Community Centre keeps a library, runs a newsletter service and provides amenities for social intercourse and entertainment. It is a well-funded and efficiently-run business. In 1988 I was invited to attend a 'Noite de Fado' in the club-bar of their community hall. Appearing that evening was Manoel Cascareijo, an amateur Fadista then in his sixties who had spent over half his life in California, but had sung the Fado on the streets of Lisbon as a teenager. He was supported by a quartet of instrumentalists, young Portuguese-American men, who had honed their art to a level of astonishing ability. They opened the recital with several intricate and flawlessly executed instrumentals, prompting the record-company executive, with whom I had driven down from San Francisco, to comment 'I'm ready to record these guys.' Manoel Cascareijo took the microphone, accepted the applause of his friends and sang several old, traditional Fados, each accorded the proper silence and each applauded enthusiastically as it closed. Yet, for all the similarity of this night to those I had experienced in Lisbon there was a real difference, and essentially it was an economic one. Here, in San Leandro, there was no grinding poverty evident. People were living the good life that Miss Sumares commented on in 1942. The mood, therefore, was one of benign and comfortable nostalgia rather than of a necessary catharsis.

The people in the centre that night were almost overwhelmingly welcoming. I talked at length with a large group of them about life in Portugal and California, culture shock, the Fado, saudades and politics. The impressions I came away with were that while the older people loved America deeply, homesickness constantly nagged at them. Manoel Cascareijo, nearing retirement, was planning to go home. He wanted to end his days in Lisbon, where he had started, but he spoke without regret of the time spent in California. Life had not been easy, but it had been immeasurably better than it could have been at home. Now, however, it was time to go back. For the younger people, those born in America but brought up with a Portuguese background, the emotions were different. They regarded America as home. Some had never been to Portugal at all, and some who had said they found aspects of it difficult to cope with. There were others who were fascinated by the 'old country', and either visited it frequently and loved it or badly wanted to see it for the first time. One young guitarrista, born in San Francisco, was planning to relocate in Lisbon within two years and become a professional musician. They all agreed, however, that Portugal was their spiritual homeland and that even the most Americanized of them still felt and understood saudade.

Fado in Brazil

Covering an area of over three million square miles, Brazil is the single largest Lusophone country in the world, and its population greater by far than the rest of the world's Portuguese-speaking communities measured together. Viewed in Portugal as the 'new world', it was long regarded as the place to migrate to, the promised land, more so than North America, since the cultural and linguistic markers shifted far less for the newly-arrived immigrant. This is perhaps the main reason why, compared to Italians, Russians or Irish, for example, the numbers of Portuguese immigrants into the United States were relatively limited; they had their own America to go to. By the time Emperor Dom Pedro had been replaced with a republican government in 1889, Brazil was a vibrant country with a rich mixture of cultures freely interacting with each other, and the two major cities, Rio de Janeiro and São Paulo, could boast amenities to rival Paris and New York.

Brazilian society comprised a cultural blend of indigenous, European and African roots that allowed the parallel development of a number of musical genres. In the latter part of the nineteenth century, Brazil produced the Maxixe, a syncretic dance that owed as much to Carribean influence as it did to European. By 1915 a prototype Samba was being developed in Rio, which reached the general public two years later with the recording of Ernesto dos Santos's 'Pelo Telefone', by Banda Odeon, and generally acknowledged as the first record to feature a Samba rhythm. Both dances were regarded as wholly Brazilian inventions, and with the advent of the annual Rio Carnaval, the multi-racial Samba became emblematic of Brazilian culture. As a result, the transplanted Fado lived in its shadow, surviving only into the first half of the twentieth century.

Initial evidence of the Fado in Brazil can be found in the recordings made by an artist called 'Bahiano', who, accompanied by a solo guitarra, sang 'Fado Português' and 'Fado Soldado' for the Zonophone company in either 1903 or 1904. Between then and 1925, when the Western-Electric recording system arrived, the recorded Fado heard in Brazil was strikingly similar to that of Lisbon and Porto, a mix of revista hits and a few solo artists. Between 1926 and 1935, although only a handful of Fadistas were actually recorded in Brazil, a good many Portuguese-recorded Fados appeared on the Brazilian market. The infrastructure of the record industry in Brazil was essentially the same as in North America. The HMV recordings were issued by the Victor company, who had a semi-autonomous office in Rio, and both Columbia and Odeon recordings, locally manufactured, appeared on their own logos. Artists such as Ercília Costa, Edmundo de Bettencourt, Armandinho, Artur Paredes and Adelina Fernandes all had their records issued in Brazil, often to coincide with and promote a tour.

By 1935, however, the local market was supporting only a hard core of resident Fadistas who catered to the ex-patriot Portuguese community, those who, perhaps, suffered the keenest pangs of saudade. The most popular of these was Manoel Monteiro, a smooth-voiced singer with crystal-clear diction, whose career lasted over 25 years. He sang of the pain of leaving the old country, of the readjustments necessary in the new, of the saudade felt by the immigrant. His style, based upon the classic Lisbon sound, was often augmented by the addition of a second guitarra and a viola-baixo, creating a deeper, louder and brighter performance. He was immensely popular, and from 1933 until 1944 the Odeon company, for whom he exclusively recorded, issued one coupling by him almost every month. They then appear to have dropped him from their roster, and he remained obscure until five years later when the locally-owned Todamerica label began recording him, continuing until his retirement in 1959.

During Monteiro's timeframe, some 50 other Fadistas made local recordings, but none so extensively. Only Isalinda Serramota, who was active for most of the 1930s, recorded more than just a handful of songs. Compared with the huge output of other Brazilian music, the Fado represented a footnote in the country's musical history and, with the advent of the Bossa-Nova in the late 1950s, the popularity of the Fado went into steep decline. Perhaps the need for assimilation, or maybe the rewards offered by it, stunted the Fado's growth in Brazil, but whatever the reason, it had largely fallen from view by the mid-1960s.

* * *

In those parcels of land that had long been a part of the Empire, and where the

Portuguese language and culture prevailed, the Fado was as much a part of every-day life as it was in the homeland. Thus it is unsurprising to find Ercília Costa, Armandinho and Adelina Fernandes appearing in Madeira and the Azores, where support for the Fado has always been strong and local Fadistas can still find work singing in restaurants today. There is also some evidence of expeditions to more isolated destinations. Mozambique was visited by, among others, Berta Cardosa and Armandinho, in the company of instrumentalists João da Mata and Martins D'assunção, in 1933. Recorded Fado was available in all these places, and also in Macao and Goa, where they were broadcast on local radio. Wherever there has been a significant Portuguese community, both resident and visiting Fadistas have always been welcome. Evidence of a market for the Fado abroad has also been gathered from its appearance in record catalogues published in Britain, France, Germany, Spain, Italy, Egypt and Canada, and one of the most frequent names to appear has been Amália Rodrigues.

Following her triumphant 1960 Paris concert, Rodrigues spent two years work-ing in São Paulo almost continuously. She then devoted much of the next quarter-century to travelling the world. In 1962 she sang in Madrid and Angola, appeared at the Edinburgh festival in September, accompanied by Domingos Camarinha and Castro Mota, and then travelled directly to Paris for a simultaneous two-month engagement at the Tête De L'Art and the ABC theatre. The following year she visited London, Beirut, Cannes and Paris again. Throughout the next 25 years she appeared in Mozambique and Angola; in Tel Aviv, Haifa and Jerusalem; in Rio de Janeiro and São Paulo, Montevideo, Santiago and Buenos Aires; in South Africa and Rhodesia; in New York, Los Angeles, Newport, Toronto, Ottawa and Montreal; in London, Brussels, Paris, Cannes, Geneva, Lausanne, Montreux, Palermo, Amsterdam, Barcelona, Madrid, Berlin, Athens, Rome, Milan, Venice and Bucharest; in Osaka and Tokyo; in Leningrad, Moscow, Tiflis and Baku, and in Beirut. Many venues were visited time and again. Her appearances in Paris and New York especially were almost annual.

The impact of this constant and highly successful touring, backed by the mar-keting that accompanied it, did far more for the profile of Portugal in general and the Fado in particular than any other single factor. Because of Amália, the sound of the Fado is known around the world, but also because of her success, that sound altered from the 1960s onwards to become often lushly orchestrated and commercialized. Purists grumbled that she had abandoned her roots[9] but then she would take them by surprise and produce authentic, heartfelt Fados of great purity. Nevertheless, the world's image of Portuguese music was largely based upon the more commercial offerings that Amália produced.

Amália slipped into semi-retirement in the late 1980s, and now lives quietly in Lisbon with her husband. She remains an icon of and for the Portuguese and whatever criticisms may be levelled against her by old-guard purists she is un-deniably the most successful musician Portugal has ever produced. In the 1950s, when American music was at its most influential in Europe, the Fado may have sunk into oblivion. Instead, the artistry of Amália Rodrigues and her contemporaries inspired the post-war generation to both listen to and practise the Fado, and thus ensure for it a significant place in musical history.

Notes

1. *The Voice of Victor*, June 1912.
2. *The Voice of Victor*, July 1920.
3. *The Voice of Victor*, May 1922.
4. *The Voice of Victor*, April 1923.
5. *Phonographic Monthly Review*, various issues, 1929–30.
6. Library of Congress notes by Sidney Robert Cowell, 1938 and 1939.
7. Library of Congress notes by Russell Lee, 1942.
8. Author's conversations with several Portuguese-Americans between 1987 and 1989.
9. Ibid.

Glossary and Gazetteer

ALENTEJANO   Rural area due east of Lisbon, abutting the Spanish frontier

ALFAMA   Old quarter of Lisbon, below St George's castle

BAILADO   Dance (noun)

BAILE   Dance (verb)

BAIRRO ALTO   'High Barrio', an area immediately above the Roçio, reached by funicular tram

BANDOLIM   Lusophone mandolin. Sometimes applied to the tenor mandolin

BATUQUE   Archaic Afro-Brazilian dance form

BEIRA-BAIXA   Sparsely populated area in the north of Portugal

BICA   Neighbourhood of Lisbon, abutting the docks

CANTIGA   Generic term for a ballad or popular song

CAVAQUINHO   Four-stringed ukulele-like instrument with 17 frets, generally tuned D-G-B-D

CHARAMBA   Brazilian dance

CHOUPAL   A wide, tree-lined walkway in Coimbra

CHULA   Rural dance of Northern Portugal

DECIMA   A ten-line quatrain

DESAFIO   Poetic improvisational singing contest, often competitively ribald in nature

DOURO   The river running through the north of Portugal, in the wine country

ESCUDO   The main unit of Portuguese currency

ESTILO   'In the style of'; used to denote that a song is being sung in a characteristic fashion

ESTUDANITA   Small ensemble of string and wind instrumentalists

FADO-CANÇÃO   Literally, 'fate song', a generally more popularized version of the Fado that grew in popularity from the 1940s onwards

FADO-CORRIDO   A specific form of Fado that is either topical or historic in content

MATRIX	The original recording from which all copies are pressed (pl: Matrices)
MAXIXE	Fusion of the Cuban Habanara, Brazilian Lundum, Argentinian Tango and Polish Polka, created in the late nineteenth century and popularized in Rio de Janeiro
MINHO	Region of Northern Portugal
MOURARIA	Literally, 'Moorish Area', one of the old quarters of Lisbon
OCARINA	Small hand-held wind instrument, made of stone, with several blow-holes
POUSADA	Traditional Portuguese restaurant
QUATRAIN	Four line rhyming couplet in song form
RAMALDEIRA	Traditional dance of Northern Portugal
REIS	Decimal division of the Escudo (qv)
ROÇIO	The main square in the centre of Lisbon
REBETIKA	Urban Greek music of the Athens underworld
RHUMBA(RUMBA)	Traditional Cuban dance, subsequently popularized worldwide
SAMBA	Brazilian dance and song form
SANTA CLARA	Ancient convent in Coimbra
SÉ VELHA	Ancient church in Coimbra celebrated for its romantic architecture
SON	Cuban song form
TANGO	Argentinian urban song and dance form, later gaining worldwide popularity
TUNA	A term used in Coimbra for a large group of musicians, generally playing string instruments
VIRA	Rural dance of Northern Portugal
WAX	Factory-produced test pressings of 78rpm records

Bibliography

Beckford, William (1928), *Travel Diaries*, London.

Bell, Aubrey (1915), *Portugal and the Portuguese*, London.

Bradford, Sarah (1969), *Portugal & Madeira*, London: Ward Lock.

de Brito, Joaquim Pais (1994), *Fado Voices and Shadows*, Lisbon: Electa.

de Carvalho, Pinto (1904), *Historia do Fado*, Don Quixote; reprinted 1984, Lisbon: Contexto.

de Sousa, Afonso (1986), *O canto e a Guitarra na Década de Oiro de Academia de Coimbra*, Coimbra.

Dos Santos, Vitor Pavão (1987), *Amália – Uma Biografia*, Lisbon: Contexto.

Ellingham *et al.* (1994), *Rough Guide to Portugal*, London: Rough Guides.

Elwes, Alfred (1891), *A Dictionary of the Portuguese Language in Two Parts*, London: Crosby Lockwood.

Gallop, Rodney (1931), 'Some Records of the Portuguese Fado', *The Gramophone*, October.

Gallop, Rodney (1936), *Portugal – A Book of Folkways*, Cambridge: CUP.

Gordon, Jan & Cora (1934), *Portuguese Somersault*, London: Harrap.

Jackson, Lady Catherine (1874), *Fair Lusitania*, London.

Livermore, H.V. (1966), *A New History of Portugal*, Cambridge: Cambridge University Press.

McCaul, Lawton (1931), *Portugal For Two*, NYC: Dodd, Mead & Co.

Pimental, Alberto (1904), *A Triste Canção do Sul*, Lisbon.

Ribeiro, José Caiel (1926), *O Fado*, Oporto.

Rosario, Antonio (1992), *Fados – Cançoes*, Lisbon: self-published.

Sucena, Eduardo (1992), *Lisboa, o Fado e os Fadistas*, Portugal: Veda.

Taylor, James L. (1970), *A Portuguese-English Dictionary*, CA: Stanford UP.

Vernon, Paul (1995), *Ethnic & Vernacular Music 1898–1960*, CT: Greenwood Press.

Discography

Label & Cat. No.	Artist & Title	Format & Vintage
ACCORD		
401132	Amália Rodrigues – Fados	[CD] c. 1970s
ARIOLA (Portugal)		
74321182674	Carlos Zel–Fados	[MC] 1993
DISCOSETTE (Portugal)		
C-636	Argentina Santos – A Rir, A Brincar	[MC] 1989
1089-4	Argentina Santos – Meu Fado	[MC] 1995
EMI-VALENTIM DE CARVALHO (Portugal)		
7243 8 31965 2 4	Various Artists – Biografia do Fado	[2CD]1929–1960
7243 8 34618 2 0	Dr António Menano – Fados V.1	CD 1927–1929
7243 8 36445 2 0	Dr António Menano – Fados V.2	CD 1927–1929
7243 8 37495 2 2	Dr António Menano – Canções	CD 1927–1929

Label & Cat. No.	Artist & Title	Format & Vintage
EMI (International)		
HEMIMDCD100	The Story of the Fado	CD 1930s–1960s
EMI (UK)		
7243 82844228	Amália Rodrigues – Live in Brasil	[CD] 1972
7243 83065127	Amália Rodrigues – Cheiga a Lisboa	[CD] 1994
EPM (France)		
995502	Various Artists – Fados	[CD] 1940s 1950s
995782	Amália Rodrigues – The First Recordings	[CD] 1945
ESTORIL (Portugal)		
200009–2	Various Artists – Fados e Desgarradas	[CD] 1950s
FMS (Germany)		
2041	Pedro Caldeira Cabral – Guitarra Portuguesa	[CD] 1994
HERITAGE (UK)		
HTCD09	Various Artists – Portuguese String Music	[CD] 1908–1931
HTCD14	Various Artists – Fados de Lisboa	[CD] 1928–1936
HTCD15	Various Artists – Fados de Coimbra	[CD] 1926–1930
HTCD24	Various Artists – As Fadistas de Lisboa – Lisbon Women singers	[CD] 1928–1931

Label & Cat. No.	Artist & Title	Format & Vintage
HTCD25	Armandinho – the HMV sessions	[CD] 1928
HTCD31	Dr António Menano	[CD] 1927–1928
HTCD32	Ercília Costa with Armandinho	[CD] 1931

MONITOR (USA)

	Amália Rodrigues live at The Olympia, Paris	[CD] 1960

MOVIEPLAY (Portugal)

37003	Anita Guerrero	[CD]
37005	Carlos Do Carmo	[CD]
37006	Fernanda Batista	[CD]
37011	Luis Picarra/Domingues Marques	[CD]
37014	Vicente de Camara/Maria Terese De Noronha	[CD]
37015	Maria de Lourdes Resende	[CD]
37020	Rui de Mascarenas	[CD]
37024	Vicente de Camara	[CD]
37025	Fernanda Maria	[CD]
37031	Fernando Farinha	[CD]
37033	Maria de Fé	[CD]
37036	Carlos & Artur Paredes	[CD] 1970s
37044	Herminia Silva	[CD] 1940s
37045	Various – Fados de Coimbra	[CD]
SO3006	Fernando Farinha – 50 Anos do Fado	[CD] 1992

NB: Except where noted, the recording dates of Movieplay releases are unknown, but are likely to be mostly from the 1970s.

MUSIC OF THE WORLD

CD12502	Amália Rodrigues – Coimbra	[CD] 1992

Label & Cat. No.	Artist & Title	Format & Vintage
53289	Mario Marques – Guitarra do Portugal	[CD]
NONESUCH		
79203–2	Carlos Paredes – Guitarra Portuguesa	[CD]
OCORA (France)		
559041	Fernando Machado Soares	[CD] 1988
PLAYASOUND (Portugal)		
65704	Lucilia Do Carmo – Parfum do Fado	[CD] 1977
85703	Rodrigo – Parfum do Fado	[CD] 1977
SMITHSONIAN FOLKWAYS (USA)		
40435	Musical Traditions of Portugal	[CD] 1950s
SOUNDS OF THE WORLD		
90107	Amália Rodrigues – Rainha do Fado	[CD] 1992
	PRE-RECORDED VIDEO TAPES	
A Severa	Dina Teresa	1931
Fado – História D'uma Cantadeira	Amália Rodrigues	1947
O Muido da Bica	Fernando Farinha	1963
O Pátio das Cantigas	Maria Clara	1941

Useful Addresses

Portugal
Bertrand Livraria
Rua Garret 73–75
1200 Lisboa
[Books]

Casa Amália
Rua do Carmo 56
Lisboa
[Records]

Lisvendas
Travessa San Domingos de Benfica 10, 1-esq
1500 Lisboa
[Video distributors for the film *A Severa*]

Lusomundo Filmes
Praça da Alegria 22 1o
1294 Lisboa
[Video distributors for the film *Amália – Historia D'uma Cantadeira*

Valentim de Carvalho, Lda.
Roçio
Lisbon
[Records, books, video]

United Kingdom
Red Lick Records
Porthmadog
Gwynedd
Wales, UK
LL49 9DJ
Tel. 01766 512151
[Mail order compact discs]

USA
Furtado Imports
1412 E Santa Clara St
San Jose
CA 95116
[Portuguese records, books, videos]

Pimentel's
1659 Acushnet Ave
New Bedford
MA 02746
[Portuguese records, books, videos]

Currently Active Fado Houses

In Lisbon and surrounding areas:
Adega do Ribatejo
Rua Diario de Noticias 23

Adega Machado
Rua do Norte 91
Tel. 01-36 00 95

Café Luso
Travessa da Queimada 10
Tel. 01-36 28 89

A Cesaria
Rua Gilberto Rola 20 (in Alcántara)

Fado Menor
Rua das Praças 18 (in Santos)

Lisboa a Noite
Rua das Galvaes 69
Tel. 01-36 85 57

Mile a Cem
Travessa da Espera

Painel do Fado
Rua de São Pedro de Alcántara 65

Perreirinha de Alfama
Beco do Espirito Santo 1
Tel. 01-86 82 09

Senhor Vinho
Rua das Praças
Tel. 01-36 40 06

A Severa
Rua das Gaveas 51
Tel. 01-36 00 95

Timpanos
Rua Gilberto Rola 16 (in Alcántara)

In Coimbra
Bar Diligencia
Travessa da Rua Nova

Café Santa Cruz
Praça 8 de Maio

Index

Portuguese names will be found under the first letter of the surname, omitting the prefix 'de'. Thus, de Bettencourt will be found under B, not D